step-by-step
FABRIC
PAINTING

I dedicate this book to all my students, the people who work with me and those who helped me to finish it, and thank them for all their enthusiasm, hard work, empathic sharing and friendship. I am privileged to be surrounded by such wonderful people whom, when all is said and done, I can call my friends.

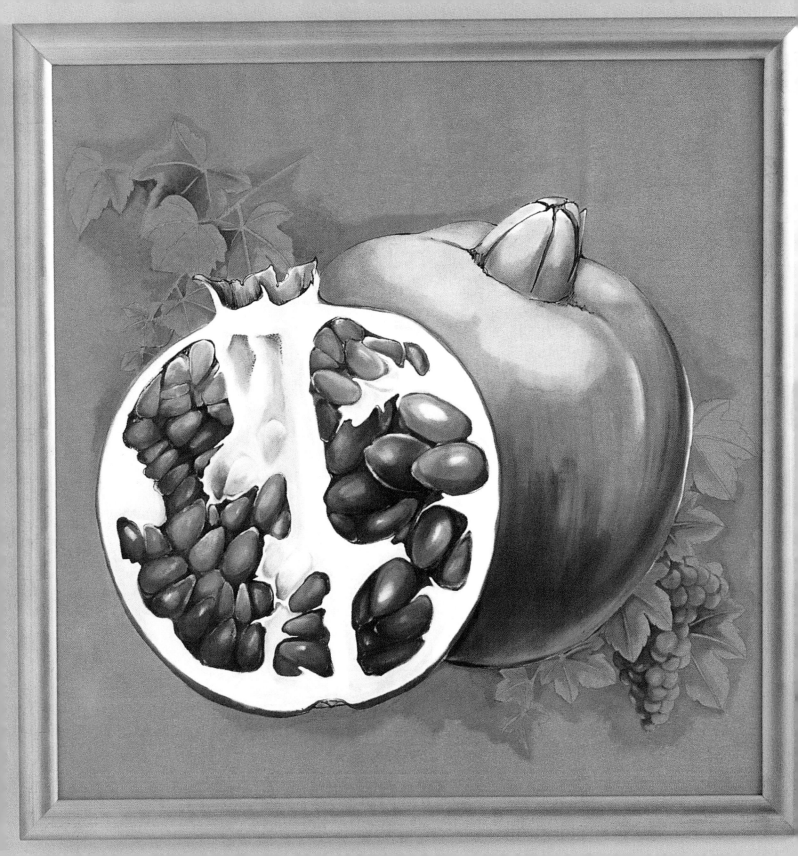

tharina odendaal
and anika pretorius

step-by-step
FABRIC
PAINTING

CONTENTS

INTRODUCTION

In this book I have used various well-known painting techniques, both on their own and in combination with others, on a number of different fabrics to create new, modern decorations for the home. We will first have a look at a couple of basic principles that must always be applied when painting on fabric. Then we will look at the different techniques used and the effect created on different kinds of fabric. Lastly, we will look at examples of interesting projects.

The techniques that will be discussed in this book are the various techniques of painting, stencilling and lastly silkscreen printing, which flows directly from stencilling. I have tried to offer something for every taste and for the different levels of skill, so there are easy projects for beginners and more difficult projects for those who are already familiar with fabric painting.

It is my wish that this book will inspire you to make your own designs and to tackle new, innovative projects, so that in the end you will develop your own style. Never before in history have we been so free to throw the rules overboard and try new things. The result is that people are now prepared to be adventurous, and they sometimes discover qualities in themselves that they did not even know they had. I hope that you, too, will soon be part of that creative group.

And, remember, if your fabric-painting project does not work, it is not the end of the world, and you should give it another try. Last, but not least, age has nothing to do with creativity – some of my best students have discovered in their golden years that they can draw, design and paint.

THARINA ODENDAAL

REQUIREMENTS

Just as with any other hobby, there are a

couple of basic pieces of equipment you will

need before you can start painting on fabric. Fortunately, these items are

cheap and, to start with, you can make do with the minimum. First learn to

master the different techniques and then buy the luxury items as and when

you need them. In this chapter, there is a

list of articles that you will generally need –

as well as a few useful tips about making

certain items yourself.

BRUSHES

Ordinary flat pig-bristle brushes work well when applying paint to fabric. The harder and stiffer the brushes, the better. Buy no. 2, 5 and 10 brushes to start off with. It is also useful to purchase one very thin paintbrush for fine detail. Extend the life of your brushes by washing them well after use with dishwashing liquid. You can also rejuvenate old brushes by cutting their bristles shorter and by thinning them out to the bottom by shaving the bristles with a razor blade.

SCRAPERS

You use scrapers to paint large flat areas or broad borders, as well as for the painting technique where a whole piece of fabric is covered with random blocks in different colours. You can buy scrapers at hardware shops – they are normally used to apply tile adhesive and are smooth on one side and serrated on the other. If you can't manage to get hold of scrapers for some reason or another, you can cut up pieces of hard cardboard into different widths, or you can even use old credit cards.

X-RAY FILMS OR SHEETS OF HARD PLASTIC

Use old X-ray films or hard sheets of plastic bought at stationery shops as a guide when scraping borders or to make pattern templates. Clean old X-rays, if necessary, by soaking them in a strong solution of bleach and then scrubbing them with a nailbrush.

SPONGES

Use sponge blocks to smooth out and round off scraped borders or the background of your design. You'll need the sort of sponges used in the kitchen or those that are used as packaging material.

You can also use sheets of sponge about 1 cm thick to cover the whole work surface. They absorb the excess paint and protect the work surface. They also ensure that the fabric you are working on does not shift around while you are painting. Firmly attach the sponge to the table using thumb tacks.

When you start painting, your most essential requirements are a sponge, a scraper, flat pig-bristle brushes and X-ray films.

ADHESIVE SPRAY

Most art shops sell this glue, which is sprayed very lightly onto the work surface to prevent slippery fabric, such as silk or organza, from shifting around. Also spray it lightly on stencils for the same reason.

Use this adhesive spray very sparingly because if you use too much it will form droplets that will leave unsightly marks on the painted fabric.

DRAWING REQUIREMENTS

Keep the following drawing items within easy reach of your work table: a couple of pencils; erasers; a long, undamaged ruler without chips (measured in centimetres); a measuring tape; different coloured pens with indelible ink; paper for notes and designs; scissors; cellophane paper on which to trace your designs and in which to pack your products; masking tape and outliners (plastic squeeze bottles containing fabric paint) for drawing.

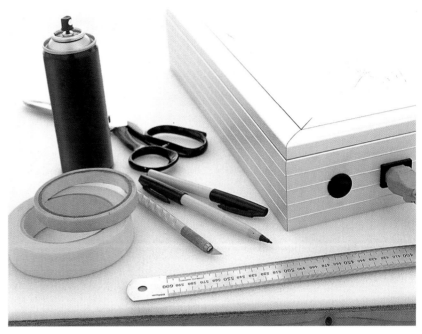

Adhesive spray, scissors, masking tape, marking pens, a ruler and a light-table must always be close at hand in your workroom.

LIGHT-TABLE

Although a light-table is very useful for drawing designs onto the fabric, it is not essential. They are available in different sizes; but rather get the largest size you can afford because it is so much easier to plan the designs on a big one than on a small one.

You can also make your own light-table by placing a large, rectangular piece of thick, clear glass with each of its short sides on the edge of a table or dresser, with a light under the glass. If the glass is too thin, however, the heat of the light will crack it.

THE WORK SURFACE

Any flat surface is suitable for working on. A large table is very useful for painting large articles such as tablecloths, while for smaller articles such as serviettes and place mats it's better to use a flat piece of wood or a tray on your lap. Then again a drawing board, or even an easel with a large board covered with sponge, on which the fabric can be attached with large paper clips, works well for painting wall hangings, paintings and blinds. Take care, however, that the table is neither too high nor too low when you are standing and working, or you could easily get backache. Cover any surface you want to work on with a layer of sponge about 1 cm thick. This absorbs any paint that may seep through the fabric and smudge the back and ensures that the fabric does not move around.

THE FABRIC

When you paint on fabric, your choice of fabric is very important. The eventual choice usually depends on what you have in mind for the end product, as the purpose of the article as well as the effect you wish to create both play a role.

Paint reacts differently on different types of fabric. On some fabrics it is very difficult to achieve a smooth effect, while on the other hand these very same fabrics may be exactly right for emphasizing your brushstrokes or an interesting texture. On other fabrics the paint flows further than the point where it was applied with a brush, and this too has a specific effect.

It is therefore very important to take note of the way the fabric you want to use is woven, and what it is woven from, before you undertake a new project. Usually, I don't work with fabrics made solely of synthetic cloth, because the painted design cannot be fixed by heat, and the colours also do not show as bright and clear as they do on fabrics of natural origin. Some fabric is also suitable only for articles that will never be washed, such as for an item that will be framed, and not for everyday household articles that regularly land in the washing machine.

Preparation of the fabric

When you buy fabric, take note that natural fabrics such as pure cotton and linen often shrink when they become wet. Therefore, always buy at least 10 per cent more fabric than you need.

Thoroughly wash all fabrics with soap in the washing machine at maximum temperature, except, of course, for organza and silk, which lose their natural gloss in the wash. This process is necessary to remove all starch, marks and impurities and to shrink the fabric before use. Hang the washed fabric outside until almost dry, then iron it thoroughly with a very hot iron.

Keep the fabric away from any paint until the design has been drawn onto it. Remember, dirt on the fabric cannot be disguised by paint and this could ruin a lovely article.

Also cut the fabric square before drawing the design on it. You cannot remedy a skew piece of fabric with a design on it by pulling or cutting it correctly later on.

PAINT

When you buy paint it is very important that it is clearly marked for use on fabrics and textiles. If the containers in which the paint is bought are not marked very clearly, rather leave them.

Textile paint is water-soluble, odourless, nontoxic and very easy to work with. The fabric paint normally used consists of two components, namely a white emulsion or transparent base (extender), which looks like joiner's glue, and a pigment, which looks like coloured ink. You can buy the paint ready-mixed to the required colour, or you can buy the emulsion and pigment separately and mix them together yourself. Nowadays, however, it is almost unnecessary to mix the colours yourself, because every imaginable shade is available ready-mixed. I prefer, however, for my students to mix their own paint – especially when they are just starting to paint – because they gain valuable experience from doing so and it makes their work more interesting.

Because I use a lot of paint, I always buy only a few basic colours and plenty of white transparent base and mix all the colours I need for a project myself. Should you run out of paint while you are painting, you can then confidently mix your own colours. Remember, however, always to mix enough paint when you are tackling a large project, because no matter how carefully you follow the recipe for a particular colour, there will undoubtedly always be a visible difference in colour.

I use the polystyrene containers in which vegetables and other food items are packed either as a palette or for mixing small amounts of paint. You can also use baby food bottles for storing small quantities of paint. When I need to mix large quantities, I use old ice-cream or margarine containers. Just remember to seal them well after you take out paint to work with. Paint that stands open becomes sticky and will have to be thrown away.

A variety of fabrics and a wide range of fabric paints will ensure that your finished products are always interesting and unique.

DESIGNS

When you paint on fabric for the first time, it is advisable to first use the patterns that

appear at the back of this book, until you have mastered the techniques. Later on, you

will probably start designing your own patterns, so be on the lookout for new ideas.

Nature is usually our greatest source of inspiration. Look at all the different kinds and shapes of leaves, flowers, tree trunks as well as textures, colours and shapes of stones, mountains, shells and even clouds in the sky.

It is also important to look at other works of art and artforms. Visit an art museum or a few art exhibitions and take particular notice of the great variety of designs, colours and textures.

Also study a few flowers and leaves in your garden and then try to draw them. Try to reproduce exactly what you see and experience, because this is precisely the mystery of art – each person sees something quite different or experiences it in a unique way.

After you have made a couple of sketches, you can enlarge the design on paper before eventually tracing it onto the fabric.

This sketch formed the basis for the design of the mushrooms on fabric in the picture alongside.

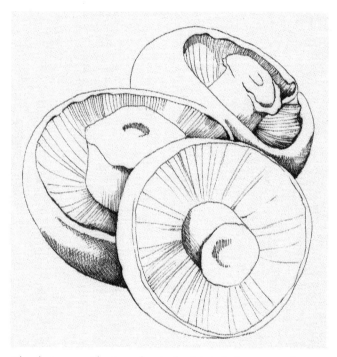

The design must be traced onto the fabric before any paint can be applied.

ENLARGING AND REDUCING DESIGNS

Most of the designs featured on pages 112–126, as well as those that must be copied from the photographs shot directly from above, for example the magnolia design on page 85, are not the correct size and will need to be enlarged. The easiest and quickest way of enlarging designs is by using a photocopying machine. Unfortunately, it's not always possible to get the required size on an ordinary machine and the design sometimes has to be repeatedly enlarged until it's the right size. Some of the larger towns and cities have facilities available to get any desired size, but it is quite costly.

An alternative plan that works well if you have an over-head projector available is to make a transparency of the design and project it onto a wall to which paper has been firmly pasted. You can then easily enlarge the design to the desired size by moving the projector. Just make sure that the projector throws the image plumb against the wall, or else you'll have a distorted image. If it is possible to secure the fabric flat against the wall, you can then trace the design directly onto the fabric.

APPLYING DESIGNS TO FABRIC

After you have drawn the design to the desired size on paper with a black pen, you can trace it onto the fabric. Depending on the pattern and the effect you want to create in the end product, you can trace the pattern on the fabric with a pencil, different coloured indelible ink pens, or you can use plastic squeeze bottles filled with fabric paint for drawing (outliners). You usually use a pencil when you want a very soft effect. Black ink looks much harder than navy blue, for instance, but even colours like dark red and bottle green look wonderful for the outlines of an object.

If you are right-handed it works very well if you start to trace the design at the top left-hand corner. In this way you will not smudge the wet ink or paint with your hand. If, on the other hand, you are left-handed, it's a good idea to start painting in the top right-hand corner, for the same reason. Sometimes, however, depending on the design, it's easier to start in the middle.

The ideal way of tracing the design onto the fabric is by working on a light-table. The pattern shows up clearly on the light-table and is thus very easy to trace. If, however, you do not have a light-table or cannot improvise one (see page 11), there are several other methods of tracing the pattern onto the fabric:

1 Place the pattern, which has been drawn on white paper, under the fabric and trace it with a fabric marker. If the pattern is drawn very clearly, it works well on white or any light-coloured fabric. Do not, however, make any unnecessary marks on the fabric when you are working with a pencil, because it is very difficult to erase pencil marks from fabric.

2 Another very effective way of tracing a pattern neatly is to place dressmaker's carbon paper on top of the fabric and under the pattern. The pattern can then be traced, even with an empty ballpoint pen, since the carbon comes off on the fabric when pressed. This method is usually used on dark-coloured fabrics that are not transparent. In the case of dark-coloured fabrics, white carbon paper is used.

3 If you need to trace a relatively small design onto a small piece of fabric and you cannot make another arrangement, you can use natural light to trace the design onto the fabric. Place the paper pattern on a clear glass windowpane with the fabric on top, then trace the design.

COLOUR

Colour can make a weak design great or it can break a good design. Experiment and play with colour. The time spent on this is an investment and can save you a lot of disappointment later on.

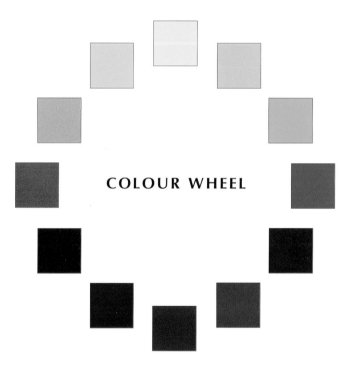

COLOUR WHEEL

The colour wheel is a very handy device for putting colour combinations together.

First play around a bit with your paint so that you get a feel for colour before you start on a design. Take yellow, for instance, and mix it with all the basic colours to see what new colours you get. Remember to make very clear notes while you are doing this, and also paste in a bit of cloth on which the colour is painted next to each 'recipe'. Repeat the whole exercise with all the most important colours to see the colour range available to you.

If you plan to mix your own colours too, first take note of the following interesting facts about colour: Although the basic colour wheel consists of only three colours (red, yellow and blue) and it is generally accepted that all colours can be mixed from them, this is not really the case. Take, for instance, red and navy blue. If you mix these two colours you will get an ugly, dirty purple. This happens because the red leans to the yellow side of the colour wheel. The same thing occurs when you mix blue and yellow. The navy blue and yellow do make green, but not a fresh grass green or emerald green. You also cannot make red lighter to get a pretty pink.

REQUIRED COLOURS

Buy a large amount of transparent base along with the following list of colours:

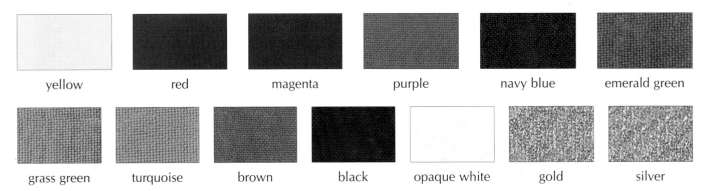

yellow   red   magenta   purple   navy blue   emerald green

grass green   turquoise   brown   black   opaque white   gold   silver

The above colours can also be mixed to make the following important colours:

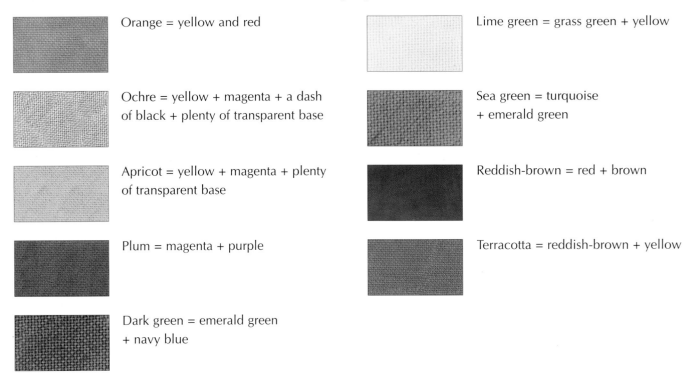

Orange = yellow and red

Ochre = yellow + magenta + a dash of black + plenty of transparent base

Apricot = yellow + magenta + plenty of transparent base

Plum = magenta + purple

Dark green = emerald green + navy blue

Lime green = grass green + yellow

Sea green = turquoise + emerald green

Reddish-brown = red + brown

Terracotta = reddish-brown + yellow

Try the following exercises to experiment with colour. Note how the examples of the plums, from left to right, can change, depending on the colours used.

Plums with blue as base colour. For lighter and darker shades of blue, add either opaque white or transparent base. The result is a very dull blue and lifeless plum.

Add a little red for a strong but lighter purplish blue. For the darker shades, add magenta and later more navy blue rather than black for a richer and warmer representation.

Now use the colours that are on opposite sides of the colour wheel, for example yellow and light orange. Then apply different shades of purple.

Be adventurous and play with colour, and do not be afraid to use contrasting colours together. Light and shadow give depth to the painting and add interest to the design.

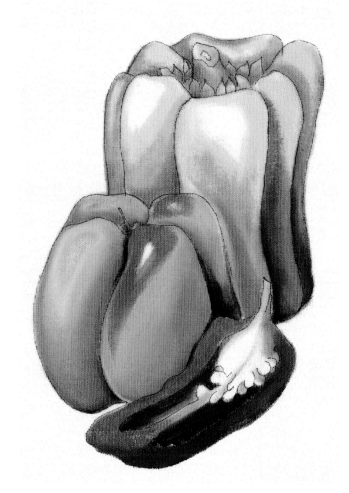

For the shades of green in the lemon leaves, add yellow to the grass green to make it lighter. For darker shades, use emerald green, and later add navy blue for the darkest greens.

To blend the different colours of different objects alongside each other, such as the different colours of peppers, use some of the colour of the yellow pepper in the green pepper, or use some of the colours in the green pepper in the red one, and vice versa.

HEAT TREATMENTS

When you use textile paint on fabric, the colours have to be fixed to make them colourfast. This means that you must employ some process or other to prevent the colours from fading as a result of exposure to light or from washing out.

Most textile paints are fixed with heat, but always read the instructions first because paints can differ. You can use the heat of an oven, tumble dryer or iron. If you want to make vast amounts of fabric colourfast, some dry-cleaners will do it for you with their big roller presses. All paint must be completely dry before any heat treatment can be applied.

IN THE OVEN

Only unprocessed painted fabric can be made colourfast in an oven, since the padding and even thread can melt from the heat. Another disadvantage of this method is that only small quantities of fabric can be treated at a time.

1 Preheat the oven to 140–170 °C (300–340 °F). Place a very thick layer of newspaper on a baking tray with the folded fabric on top, and place the rack in the middle of the oven. Make quite sure that the fabric does not hang over the edge of the paper or baking tray, since those parts will get singed and turn brown. Also make sure that the newspaper does not touch the sides of the oven as it could catch fire.

2 Leave the fabric in the oven for 5–7 minutes. If the oven light comes on during this time, lower the temperature immediately to prevent the elements from switching on.

3 If you need to make a large article colourfast, unfold and then refold it in another way and heat-treat in the oven for a second time.

IN THE TUMBLE DRYER

As with the oven method, you can only treat unprocessed fabric in this way since the padding and even the thread can be damaged by the heat.

1 Once you have made certain that all painted areas are completely dry, place the fabric in the tumble dryer at maximum heat for 30–60 minutes.

WITH AN IRON

You can also fix colours with an ordinary iron, but then you must make sure that the whole area is treated and that you hold the iron on each section long enough.

You can use this method to make finished articles colourfast. The ideal way, however, is to treat the fabric before it is processed.

1 Check to make sure that all painted areas are completely dry, then repeatedly iron the back of the fabric with the iron's temperature set on hot or 'cotton'. You should iron each painted area for at least 3 minutes.

PAINTING TECHNIQUES

The painting technique is considered as the most basic technique for painting on fabric, and when you do stencilling and silkscreen work, you also apply certain aspects of this technique. It is therefore advisable to master the painting

technique before applying any of the other techniques and before you start on a large or difficult project. Painting is more than just colouring in – it is a specific technique that creates a particular mood or conveys depth.

When we want to impart colour to a geometric design or just want to create a simple effect with colour, we simply colour in. When we paint, however, we want to say more, to create a particular mood or convey depth.

There are many different painting techniques and one is certainly not better than another. In the course of time, each person develops his or her own technique. Some people paint more smoothly and tidily, while others work more freely and the brushstrokes are more visible.

Unfortunately, painting is not so simple that there is a recipe with step-by-step instructions that guarantee success time after time. However, I am going to provide a couple of guidelines that work for me and that you can use for most articles. The colours and shapes of the objects will vary, but the basic techniques will be similar.

The techniques discussed in this chapter form the basis for all future painting. I have not discussed all the steps of the painting technique each time for every example of the later chapters, as I have chosen rather to include more examples of interesting combinations of the techniques than repeat everything every time. So the instructions are given here as fully as possible.

Here you can see clearly that one orange has a smoother, finish than the other, but that both are equally effective.

BASIC REQUIREMENTS
- Any fabric – preferably of natural fibre
- A pen, pencil or plastic squeeze bottle (outliner) for the outlines of the design
- White pig-bristle brushes: no. 2, 4, and 6 for small designs; no. 6 and 10 for large designs
- Paint
- Containers for paint

BASIC PREPARATIONS
When you start painting it is important that you give your full attention to the painting. Therefore, make a few basic preparations before you start and provide:

1 A clean and tidy work surface. Old, dry or wet paint could smudge your new, clean cloth and wreck your whole project.

2 A clean palette and containers with clean water. A palette that is still dirty from previous paint is going to make all your new colours dirty and grainy, and dirty water also detracts from the clarity of your colours.

3 Clean brushes for painting. If you paint with a dirty brush, little particles of old paint will work loose from the bristles all the time and mix with your new, clean paint. So wash your brushes after use with hot soapy water every time.

4 A clean, soft cloth to wipe away any paint that spills or is superfluous.

COLOUR, SHAPE AND TEXTURE

Everything in nature is three-dimensional and painting must also foster the illusion of three dimensions.

When you want to paint something, you must first identify the basic shape of each object, so study the shapes of flowers, leaves, vases, cups and so on. Light and shadow also help to create the illusion of three dimensions. Light should preferably come from the side, because when it shines from the front, the design looks flat. Beginners are usually timid about using contrasts to portray light and shadow on an object, but go and have another look at nature. Look at how dark the shadows are and how light the lighter areas are. Also notice the highlights.

The warm yellow shades of the lemons stand out, while the cool blue shades make the lavender in the background disappear.

The choice of colour is just as important for objects to look three-dimensional. Bright and light colours stand out and dark colours fade into the background. Warm colours appear lighter than cold colours.

GENERAL GUIDELINES

Before you start painting for the first time, it is important for you to study the following guidelines well:

1 Use a small brush to paint small areas and a wider brush for larger surfaces.

2 Always paint light colours first because you can only make colours darker, never lighter. In exceptional cases you can paint lighter colours over dark colours, but then use opaque colours that are not transparent. In this case the dark colour is over-painted with a lighter colour.

3 Paint the lightest colours over a larger area than they are meant to cover. This will help the darker colours blend in and ensures that there is no definite boundary between the colours.

4 Leave all highlights open on the fabric so that the natural white or beige of the fabric shows through, and they need not be created with opaque white later on.

5 Always paint a whole object in one sitting so that the colours can blend naturally. In this way you prevent clear colour differences being visible. By painting colours over each other, you can create many new colours.

6 Wet paint is always darker than dry paint. If you have doubts about a colour, first test it on a remnant of the same fabric and leave it to dry.

PERSPECTIVE

When you paint a design, it usually has more than one object. The objects do not all lie next to each other, but some lie in front of or on top of each other. If you paint them all the same colour, you are going to get a very flat picture. To achieve depth you need to paint the objects in such a way that you can immediately see that one object lies in front of another.

By varying the colours of the cherries, pears and leaves, you can see that some lie in front of others.

BACKGROUND

There are many techniques for painting the background. In this book we discuss four. The first technique is for an even, plain background. Using the second technique you paint the background three-dimensionally, in the third you scrape in the background, and in the fourth you paint a stippled background with a sponge roller. You use one or more of these four techniques in all the examples, because they suit the painting technique, stencilling and silkscreen printing so well.

Even, plain background

You use this technique mostly on small areas such as small tablecloths, place mats and tea cosies, but if you paint in the background neatly and evenly, it can also look very good on larger articles. But do pay attention to the type of fabric you use. Some fabrics work better than others and usually look better because the end product has a smoother and softer texture. Test it first on a remnant of fabric and leave to dry thoroughly.

REQUIREMENTS
- Scrapers of different widths
- Brushes of different thicknesses
- Old X-ray films or hard sheets of plastic
- Masking tape of different widths
- Sponge blocks
- Paint

1 Ensure that you have enough time to paint the whole background in one session. If you stop, it will leave a definite mark that will spoil the whole article.

2 Mix enough paint to cover the whole background. Even if you mix more paint in exactly the same way as before, the colour will never be quite the same, and in such a large area it will definitely show up.

3 Choose the colours for the background very carefully, especially if you are thinking about making a border in another colour. To ensure that the colours do not flow into each other, you can create a dividing line by sticking down a strip of masking tape. Take care that the masking tape adheres very well, otherwise the paint will seep under it if it's not pressed down properly. This is not such a big problem if you are using two colours that blend well, but when you are using colours such as yellow and purple, and they mix, you get an ugly brown that usually does not suit the rest of the colours.

4 You can also use X-ray films or hard sheets of plastic to create straight boundaries between colours.

5 Mix the paint very well. If it is not well mixed, the uneven colour will show up very clearly when the scraper is pulled over it.

6 Start painting neatly with a brush those areas where you are not going to use the scraper. These will be the areas between the leaves and flowers or the borders of the design, for instance.

7 Use the scraper to scrape over the large open spaces. Stop every few minutes and rub hard over the painted surface with the sponge so that the paint is as even and

The even, plain background forms a lovely contrast to the texture of the leaves.

smooth as it can be. Gold and silver paint, however, must on no account be rubbed with the sponge, or the shine will be lost.

8 It is sometimes necessary to apply two coats of paint to the whole area. Make sure, however, that you apply the same quantity of paint over the whole area, otherwise the background will be streaky and full of marks when the paint dries.

Three-dimensional background

This technique is used to further emphasize the three-dimensional main design in the foreground.

To create the illusion of distance, do not trace in the leaves right at the back when you trace the flower and leaves in front. The leaves at the back must be painted in later.

REQUIREMENTS
- Brushes of different thicknesses
- Paint

1 When painting flowers, we want to create the illusion that they are part of a bunch, in a garden or in the countryside. You suggest the distance of the leaves that are the farthest away by the absence of outlining. The farther you go to the back, the less detail you portray. The leaves thus become less and less realistic and the veins on the leaves more and more vague.

2 To create the illusion that there are more flowers in the background, apply a lighter colour to the background than that used on the flowers in the foreground.

3 To portray the sky, use very pale blues, which can sometimes even be painted over the leaves at the back. Always try to finish painting the sky areas in one sitting to ensure a gentle and ethereal effect. If you allow the paint to dry and start painting again later on, you will notice definite watermarks on the fabric.

4 In some cases, however, you will deliberately need to let the paint dry; this is done to prevent the colours from spreading. An example of when this is done is with different leaves, where you don't want the varying shades of green to run into each other.

5 You can also achieve interesting effects by painting light, misty colours at random and letting them dry. Combinations of, for instance, pale turquoise, blue and yellow look marvellous. Allow the paint to dry very well and then dilute a little contrasting colour of paint with water until it looks almost like coloured water. Drop or splash some of this watery paint over the dried, painted areas. You can also use this method for the backs of place mats, cushions or bags to add an interesting visual effect.

Scraped background

The scraping technique is quick, easy and effective in any combination of colours. A scraped background works particularly well with silkscreen printing and is also very effective for large areas, such as curtains.

REQUIREMENTS
- Scrapers of different widths
- Paint

1 Choose and mix all the paint needed for the project before you begin painting. Remember to mix enough paint to complete the whole project. Place the different coloured paints in separate containers that are wider than the scrapers.

2 Use the lightest colour, or the colour that you want to display the most, first.

3 Press the scraper into the paint, at a slant of about 30 degrees, so that there is more paint on one side of the scraper than on the other. Pull the scraper over the fabric at the same angle you pulled it through the paint, in any direction and over any distance. The marks can be solid or broken. If the marks are uneven, they form very interesting patterns and designs over which you can scrape other colours later on.

4 First scrape over the whole area with one colour before you work with other colours. This ensures that the colour will be evenly spread and that the fabric will not be darker on one side than on the other, unless that is the way you planned it.

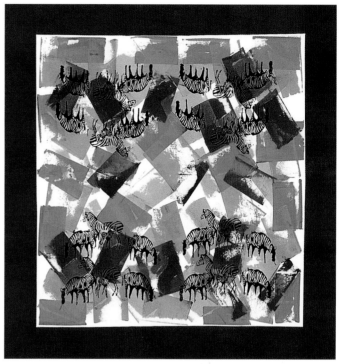

The zebras have been printed onto the fabric with black paint and a silkscreen, and the border and background have been scraped with three colours of paint.

5 Clean the scraper thoroughly before using another colour. Even if there is just a little bit of old, dry paint on the scraper, it will make a mark on your article when it becomes wet with the new paint you are applying. With this technique, you can scrape the colours over each other even when the bottom layer is still wet.

6 If, at the end, you feel that you see too little of a specific colour, scrape that colour over again.

7 You can cover the whole area with paint or you can leave open white patches on the fabric.

Stippled background

You use the same kind of roller here that you use for stencilling, except that the sponge looks as though it is full of holes. The sponges are usually yellow, are available in two different sizes and you can buy them at any hardware store. For a tablecloth, however, I prefer to use a big roller.

REQUIREMENTS
- Roller
- Paint
- Flat surface, such as an X-ray film

1 Always work on a hard, smooth surface.

2 Put a little paint on a flat surface such as an X-ray film or a hard sheet of plastic and roll the paint with the rolller until it has a very fine, even texture.

3 Now take the roller and roll it very evenly over the fabric. Do not press the roller down harder when the paint starts to run out, or the stipples will differ from one another. Rather dip your roller in the paint on the X-ray

film again and repeat the process as discussed in the previous paragraph.

4 It is quite difficult to get the stipples perfectly even, but the unevenness has its own handmade beauty.

5 You can roll more than one colour over the other, but take care that the paint is quite dry before starting with another colour.

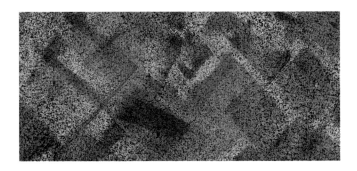

6 You can also combine stippling with the scraping technique. Just make sure that the paint is dry before starting with a new technique.

7 Wash the roller very well after use, making sure all the paint is washed out. Ensure that the sponge does not press against anything when it is packed away, or it will be partly indented when it is dry.

This technique is very easy and you can use it to create a stippled effect. It works wonderfully as a background together with a pretty border pattern in any of the other techniques.

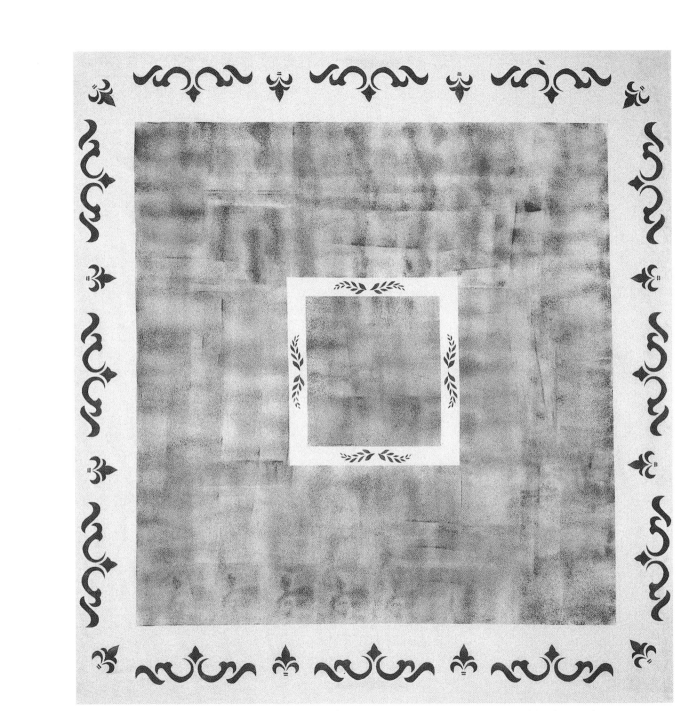

A beautiful tablecloth for a festive occasion where you combine stencilling with a stippled background.

A PLAIN BORDER

Many articles are finished off with a plain border of 4–10 cm all round. To paint this border straight and equally wide, we use X-ray films and a scraper.

How to paint the border

1 Decide how wide you want the border to be and make provision for extra fabric for the hem or the part cut off by the overlocker.

2 Make a few dots to act as a guide for the border on each side of the piece of fabric. You should preferably do this with a purple marker that washes out.

The plain border was done with a scraper and smoothed out with a sponge later on. But notice how the border does not cross the design.

3 Press the side of the X-ray film very firmly on the inside of the fabric against the dots. Start applying the paint with a scraper. Place the scraper with paint on the X-ray film and scrape it towards the material to prevent the paint getting under the film.

4 Smooth out the paint by rubbing it with a sponge. Do this specially in the corners where there will be unsightly marks because you have scraped the border from both sides.

5 Allow the border to dry completely before picking up the article and folding it.

CHECKS, STRIPES AND BLOCKS

You can use checks, stripes and blocks on their own or in combination with other designs. The choice of fabric plays an important part when you paint stripes and blocks. On some fabrics you get lovely clean lines, but on others the paint 'bleeds' and you can never get clean, sharp lines. Choose the fabric according to the effect you want to create.

Checked work with stripes, which are clearly defined.

The colours will also determine how the end product will look, and it's worth the trouble to test it on a remnant before deciding. All the stripes do not have to be the same width and also do not have to alternate evenly. The article, therefore, need not be symmetrical. You can simply start at one end and vary the colours or even just the widths of the stripes.

Colours with the same tonal value, for example just bright or just pastel colours, usually work best. Preferably use the brightest colours for the narrowest stripes. You also do not have to use all the colours in both directions. For instance, use four colours, with two in one direction and two in the other.

Checks, stripes and blocks with clean lines

In this case, you measure the stripes, checks and blocks precisely and define the lines clearly.

1 First work out the layout of the stripes, that is, the width and colours, on paper.

2 Use masking tape as a guide and to ensure clean, neat lines when you paint. Plan the stripes according to the available widths of masking tape.

3 First paste the four outlines to form a block, and then paste all the lines in one direction.

4 To make the lines equal in width, neatly stick three pieces of masking tape right next to each other. Now lift the middle strip and stick it directly against the right-hand side of the third strip. Stick another strip of tape next to this, then lift the re-used strip again. Repeat the process until you have covered the whole section.

5 Make sure that the masking tape is securely stuck down, otherwise the paint will seep under it and you will not get clean, straight lines.

6 Mix enough paint to complete the whole project, to ensure that the colours stay the same throughout.

7 Paint all the horizontal lines with a brush, scraper or sponge. Let them dry well before you stick strips of masking tape in a vertical direction to create blocks.

8 As the colours are transparent, the stripes should stop at the edge of the design, or they will show through.

Freestyle checks, stripes and blocks

In this technique, the outlines of the stripes are not always clearly defined so it is much easier to paint the stripes. You only need to use a metre rule (a ruler that is 1 m in length) as a guide and you do not have to plan the pattern beforehand.

1 Position the metre rule on the fabric and press it down firmly.

2 Use a scraper of your choice, dip it into a little paint and scrape the stripe with the metre rule as a guide. The amount of paint on the scraper will determine how solid or broken your line will be.

3 Thoroughly clean the metre rule each time you move it to a new position.

4 Place the metre rule firmly on the cloth in the next position. You can now use another colour and also a narrower or broader scraper. Repeat this process until you have covered the desired area. In other words, you then place the metre rule next to the wet stripe for the next position. Be very careful, however, not to smudge the wet paint.

5 When you have finished painting all the stripes in one direction, let the paint dry thoroughly before painting in the other direction.

6 Make sure that the stripes are still square and the same distance from the edges of the fabric by measuring every 50 cm or so to see whether you are working properly. If you start working skew, mark it and adjust the following stripes.

Checked work with stripes, which have uneven outlines.

STEP-BY-STEP EXAMPLES

Before you undertake a big project, it is perhaps advisable to paint a few simple objects first.

You could always use them as little box frames or make pot-holders of them. You will find

that you quickly become self-confident when you see how your painting is developing.

ARTICHOKE

1 Using a fine black pen, trace the design onto the fabric.

2 Decide from which side the light will fall onto the artichoke and then paint the middle parts of the leaves and stem in the lightest shade of olive green.

3 Use a darker shade of olive green and paint the leaves and stem, except where there are highlights, and the tips of the leaves, which are light green.

4 Use grass green to paint in the shadows where the leaves overlap each other and also for the side of the stem.

5 Use purple to make the shadow areas even darker, and add it here and there on the leaves to create depth.

6 You use much less green shading and more purple and magenta for the artichoke on the tablecloth. Add navy blue to the purple for the darkest areas.

Steps that show the different stages of how to paint an artichoke. Take note of how the colours are applied from lightest to darkest.

PAINT

Transparent base
Shades of olive green
Grass green
Purple
Magenta
Navy blue

BRINJAL (AUBERGINE)

1 Using a black pen, trace the design onto the fabric.

2 Decide where the highlight on the brinjal is going to be and paint around this highlight with light ochre. Also paint part of the leaves and stem with the light ochre.

3 Paint the brinjal with ochre mixed with a little magenta and lots of transparent base. Then paint light magenta over the outer part of the light ochre to give the brinjal more depth. Paint the leaves with light olive green.

4 Paint the outermost section of the brinjal with dark magenta and then with magenta that has been mixed with a little navy blue. Finish off the leaves and stem with dark olive green and a touch of light magenta here and there to add interest.

5 For a deeper purple brinjal you can start with the light magenta, continuing to make it darker and adding more and more navy blue.

PAINT
Light ochre
Transparent base
Shades of magenta
Shades of olive green
Navy blue

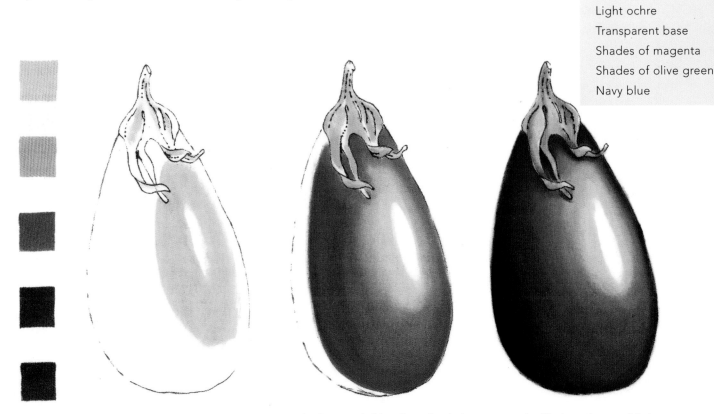

Steps that show the different stages of how to paint a brinjal. The rounded brush strokes help to create the illusion of an oval fruit.

IRIS

1 Using a pencil, draw the design onto the fabric.

2 Paint the iris using a mixture of very light magenta and yellow to paint the areas between the pencil lines that indicate the folds in the petals.

3 Then paint the different shadows at the base of the petals with a very light magenta that is almost pink.

4 First use magenta and then a mixture of magenta and navy blue to complete the petals. Paint the stem with olive green and a little dark magenta, and finish the flower with a touch of olive green here and there.

5 Irises are available in a wide range of colours, so you can use a good few different shades of the main colour to paint the flower. Create the highlights by using one very light contrasting colour.

PAINT
Transparent base
Shades of magenta
Yellow
Navy blue
Olive green

Steps that show the different stages of how to paint an iris. The paint is applied in streaks to indicate the folds on the petals.

PEA POD

1 Using a black pen, trace the design onto the fabric.

2 Use the very light yellow-green paint and paint the outlines of the half-circles at the front of the join at the top of the closed pea pod. Allow the white of the fabric to show through slightly. By doing this, you will create the illusion that there are round peas inside the closed pea pod.

3 Paint the tops of the peas with the light paint too, and leave highlights open here as well. Also use this colour for the little leaves and the parts right next to the edges of the open pod.

4 Use bright green paint to paint the rest of the pea.

5 Mix a little black with the bright green and paint the shadows between and right next to the peas, as well as on the edge of the pod.

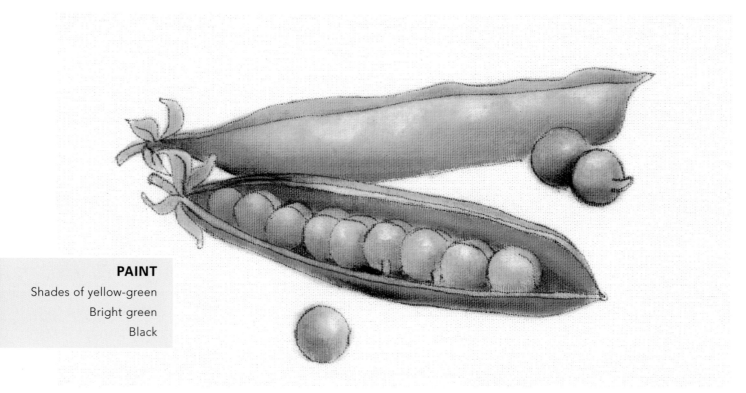

PAINT
Shades of yellow-green
Bright green
Black

A pea pod in various shades of green. The white of the fabric showing through helps to emphasize the roundness of the peas.

APPLES

For this example, step-by-step instructions have not been given, but I have pointed out certain aspects of the painting technique that can also generally be used for other designs. All the paint used here is transparent, except the white opaque paint used for the cut apple.

1 Using a fine black pen, carefully trace the design onto the fabric.

2 We start with the leaves. Notice the shape, but also the shadows on the leaves and how light and dark shades are used on the leaves to create three dimensions. Leaves are usually lighter on the underside than on the top. The parts right next to the veins are also usually darker than the rest of the leaf. The leaves in front are also lighter than the leaves at the back. The highlights are usually on the edges of the leaves. When the leaves are folded, however, the highlights fall on the highest part of the leaf – which can be in the middle of the half-leaf, for instance.

3 The use of magenta, red and shades of brown, as well as the brush strokes, help to emphasize the shape of the apple.

4 The white opaque paint used for the cut inside of the apple helps to make this part of the apple stand out. Use light shades of orange and mix it with the opaque white to paint the area around the pips.

Different tonal values help to give shape to the fruit and leaves.

PAINT

Shades of grass green
Shades of brown
Magenta
Red
Shades of orange
Opaque white

STENCILLING

Stencilling, which is considered the most primitive printing process, is the process whereby paint is applied to a surface using a cut-out pattern and a brush, roller or sponge. This process has been used

throughout the ages to decorate leather, paper, fabric and walls. For these stencils, wood, leather and metal were used, and later paper and cardboard. Today you can make your own stencils of cardboard, plastic or acetate, or you can buy ready-made stencils at some art dealers and at hobby shops.

During the 18th and 19th centuries, stencilling was highly fashionable in the rural districts of America as it was a much cheaper alternative to the wallpaper used in the homes of the wealthy. Artists travelled far and wide, decorating the interior walls of houses in exchange for board and lodging.

Nowadays, stencilling in and around the home is fashionable once again. You can apply unique borders to walls, restore an old piece of furniture, or you can make tablecloths, serviettes and curtains that all match. The technique and basic principles remain the same; it's just the paint and the surface that vary each time.

COMMERCIAL STENCILS

Beautiful commercial stencils are available today at some art dealers and hobby shops. There is a wide choice and the quality of the designs is good. By combining some of the designs, you can make new designs without trying to make your own stencils. The most common stencils are those made of mylar, which looks like white or grey plastic, and which is usually cut out by laser beam, pressed out by a punch or cut out with a drill. Then there are also tin and bronze stencils, but the designs available on this type of stencil are usually very small. Lastly, there are stencils made of paper and cardboard.

A wide range of commercial stencils are readily available, but you can make your own using an artist's knife and plastic sheets or X-ray films.

Cardboard stencils are usually not suitable for painting on fabric because they are not waterproof and, therefore, are not durable. They are also much harder to work with because they are not transparent and so are not easily placed in the right position on the fabric.

Stencils cut out by laser are very effective. They have a point registration system where little diamonds, triangles or circles are cut into each corner to indicate the precise position of each colour.

HOW TO MAKE YOUR OWN STENCIL

If you are very creative, it can be fun to make your own stencils. There are a few important points to bear in mind, however, if you want to undertake this task.

Choice of a design

You can use various leaves and flowers, as well as existing designs already present in the room, as the basis of a design. Remember, simplicity is the secret.

When you have decided on a theme for the design, it is important to choose a very good drawing or object from which to work. Place a large sheet of tracing paper over the design and start to outline the simple levels. Do not forget that there must be a little bridge between each painted area to separate one shape from the other and different colours from each other. These bridges must form part of the design, however, and enhance the effect positively, and not be just places where the design is crudely interrupted.

Since it is very difficult to use a stencil that has openings that are too large, bridges are also used to strengthen the stencil. Large openings can make the stencil very unstable and it will most likely lift and move around while you are stencilling your design.

Even one simple design can be very effective if you play with the design by repeating it or rotating it. For intricate designs, you can design two or more plates that fit over each other – one for each colour to be applied one after the other.

Materials and cutters

You can use different materials to make stencils. You can get loose sheets of plastic or acetate used for covering books at any stationery outlet. These sheets are strong and waterproof and are thus very suitable for use as stencils. You can also use well-scrubbed X-ray films to make your

In these examples, used most effectively as a border pattern, we can clearly see what is meant by the use of bridges in a stencil design. Bridges are used to show the pips and the veins of the leaves. In this case, the design is applied to the fabric with a roller and white opaque paint. Also note the difference and effect when the same pattern is used on two different kinds of fabric.

stencils, and some art shops also stock a special type of cardboard that is specifically made for stencils.

You can cut stencils with a cutter that looks like a soldering iron and works with heat. Since these cutters are very expensive and also quite difficult to use, and because they often leave a residue of ridges of melted plastic that result in uneven outlines, I prefer to use an ordinary artist's knife (also available at art shops).

Go to work as follows to make a stencil:

1 Spray the back of the material you are going to use for the stencil with adhesive spray and then stick the design you have drawn onto this material.

2 Place it on a cutting board of wood, glass or plastic or on a firm piece of cardboard.

3 Using an artist's knife, try to cut out the pattern evenly without picking it up. Turn the stencil rather than the knife and try to cut towards your body rather than away from it. Be very careful not to cut through the corners because the paint will run in there and you will not get neat, clean lines.

CARING FOR STENCILS AND STENCIL EQUIPMENT

It is very important that you always wash your stencils and brushes after use. Just one little grain of old paint can leave an ugly dark spot on a new article when it gets wet.

Store your stencils very carefully in a safe place. Make sure that they lie flat and do not become folded. Stencils are expensive and take a lot of time to make yourself and it is a difficult job to repair a torn or folded stencil.

CHOICE OF COLOURS

Traditionally, pale and muted colours were used for stencilling. Fortunately, we are more daring today and all colour combinations are acceptable.

Look at the different effects that can be achieved with different colours of paint as well as different backgrounds using the same design. Do experiment first before tackling a big project.

CHOICE OF PAINT

We usually use textile paint, oil-based crayons or acrylic paint for stencilling. Acrylic paint becomes hard and stiff and is not suitable for articles such as clothes or linen. For our purposes, therefore, we use ordinary textile paint. Also remember always to make stencilling on fabric colourfast, using the heat method to ensure washability.

PREPARING THE ARTICLE AND THE STENCIL ITSELF

From experience, I have discovered that the following preparatory steps work every time:

1 Iron the material very smoothly.

2 Spray a little adhesive spray onto a hard work surface before the fabric is placed on it and smoothed out by hand. This prevents the material from moving around while you are doing the stencilling.

3 Stick the stencil onto the fabric with masking tape or adhesive spray on the back of the stencil so that it cannot move around. Do not apply too much spray or the glue will leave marks on the fabric.

4 Clean the stencil well each time after use to prevent the paint smudging in places where you do not want it to. This is particularly important where a stencil must be turned over to create a mirror image.

STENCILLING TECHNIQUES

Brush technique

This technique is considered the traditional method of stencilling and you do it on hard surfaces. Here you will also get the familiar stippled effect. Use good-quality, flat stencil brushes for this method and use oil-based crayons or ordinary textile paint. Ordinary fabric paint is most commonly used and is also the cheapest.

1 You need very little paint for the brush technique. Pour a small quantity of paint in a bowl and lightly press the tips of the brush in it.

2 Blot off the excess paint on a piece of paper towel.

3 Keep the brush in an upright position and start to press gently on the surface of the fabric with the tip of the brush. Now paint the whole area in this way. Take care that the stencil also gets paint on it so that the design has a strong outline. To get a lighter surface, apply only a little paint. You must apply more paint to create a shadow effect, which will give your design a three-dimensional quality to your design.

4 Raise the stencil gently on one side so that you can evaluate the painting.

5 If you are satisfied with the result, you can remove the masking tape and carefully lift the stencil.

Three shades of green and two shades of brown have been used in this example, and sometimes they have been mixed to create an interesting effect.

6 Allow the paint to dry thoroughly. Then place the stencil on the next area to be painted and repeat the whole process. Take care not to be in too much of a hurry and put the stencil on wet paint if you are going to repeat the pattern. Remember, a stencil pattern that has been smudged cannot easily be rectified by simply painting over blobs of paint or enlarging flowers or leaves.

7 Don't forget to make the paint colourfast with a heat treatment if it has to be washable.

Painting technique

For this technique, you use an ordinary, flat pig-bristle brush on a hard surface. Here you can also use different colours of paint on one stencil.

1 Dip the brush into the paint. The amount of paint needed will depend on the size of the area to be painted.

2 Paint from the stencil towards the fabric, never from the fabric to the edge of the stencil, since the paint will seep under the edge.

3 Use turquoise, purple, brown and gold paint for the examples of the feather shown below.

Use brown to paint the shaft and a very small area of the feather's upper and lower sides. Then use turquoise paint for the top half of the feather and purple for the lower half. Leave parts of the inside unpainted so that the white of the fabric is visible.

Paint this feather only with gold paint, which makes it very effective on any colour background.

This feather is a combination of the previous two examples. Use only turquoise to paint the whole feather from outside to inside. Then paint the outsides of the feather purple and, lastly, apply the gold only to the sides and the shaft.

Roller technique

For this technique you will use different widths of rollers to apply the paint on a hard work surface. This is definitely the easiest and quickest stencilling technique, but it is also the most difficult to apply different shades of paint.

1 Use a dry sponge roller or wet it and squeeze the water out very well.

2 Put spoonfuls of paint on a flat surface such as an X-ray film.

3 Roll the roller over the paint.

4 Now roll the roller a couple of times over a clean area until the paint gets a very fine texture. The roller is now ready to be used on the stencil and the fabric.

5 Hold the stencil very firmly and roll over all the open areas until the desired colour has developed evenly.

6 You can put the roller into the paint again, but you must roll it over a clean area every time to get an even texture before using it on the stencil and fabric.

Two stencils were used for each of these examples – one for the vase and the other for the flowers. The stencil for the vase was used first. A wide roller was used to apply the light blue and purple paint. The left-hand vase was first painted with blue paint, then light purple was applied to the outside for a shadow effect. The right-hand vase was painted only in purple. After the paint dried very well, a second stencil was used for the decoration. A smaller roller was used to apply the decorations with opaque white paint.

Sponging technique

This technique is most suitable for beginners who do not immediately want to purchase all the requirements for stencilling and so do not want to buy extra brushes or a roller. The sponging technique is also a great deal cheaper because you use an ordinary, wet kitchen sponge to apply the paint. Just remember to first squeeze the water out thoroughly.

1 Pour the paint into a container.

2 Dip the sponge into the paint and then on paper towel to remove the excess paint.

3 Press the sponge lightly over the stencil to apply the paint to the fabric.

Sponge on the background with light bluish-purple. When the fabric is completely dry, apply the flowers to the fabric with a sponge, using reddish-purple, and the same stencil that was applied to the light bluish-purple fabric in the previous example.

VARIATIONS OF ARUM LILIES

To show how versatile stencilling can be and the different effects that you can create, we use only one stencil in the following examples, but different colours paint and stencilling techniques. Notice that the designs are really very simple and that there are not even many bridges in the design.

(a) Brown and ochre arum lilies

1 Follow the general directions for preparing articles for stencilling (see page 46).

2 Start with the lightest arum lilies at the back. Use a roller and the light ochre paint.

3 You can gradually make the stems of the arum lilies darker from the bottom with a brush.

4 Remove the stencil carefully and leave the paint to dry thoroughly.

5 Place the stencil partly over the first design and now use ochre to which you have added a little brown paint. You can again make the stems darker from the base up by adding more brown.

6 Remove the stencil and let the paint dry completely before you proceed.

7 Now place the stencil slightly lower over the earlier paint and this time use the brown paint only.

PAINT
Brown
Ochre

(b) Brown, white and green arum lilies

1 Follow the general directions for preparing articles for stencilling (see page 46).

2 Start with the white and green arum lilies at the back. Use a roller and the opaque white paint to paint in the flowers.

3 Paint the stems with a little roller and grass green paint that has been mixed with a little yellow. You can paint the stems a little darker on the outside against the stencil.

4 Using a fine brush, also paint a little green over the opaque white at the base of the flowers and a little opaque white over the green at the tops of the stems.

5 Remove the stencil carefully and leave the paint to dry completely before you proceed.

6 Place the stencil partly over the first design and now use a stencil brush and shades of brown mixed with a little ochre for the top flower. Leave faintly stippled highlights open for texture. Use brown paint for the rest of the flowers. You can make the stems a little darker from the base upwards.

7 Remove the stencil and let the paint dry very well before you do any more stencilling.

8 Again, place the stencil slightly over the first paint application and this time use the brown paint only to do the stencilling.

PAINT

Opaque white
Grass green
Yellow
Brown
Ochre

(c) White arum lilies with green stems

1 Follow the general directions for preparing articles for stencilling (see page 46).

2 Use a stencil brush and lots of light grass green and make light stipples on the stems. The parts in the middle of the stems must be less stippled so that the stems appear round.

3 Now use a brush with the darker grass green paint to paint the area directly next to the edge of the stencil and where one stem goes behind the other.

4 For the lily flowers, we use a combination of stencilling and painting techniques. Actually, the stencil serves here as the outline for the subject that is being painted. Paint the flowers by painting from the edge of the stencil towards the inside with maroon, yellow and purple paint. Paint the colours over each other where there are shadows. Lastly, paint with opaque white and leave spots open on the inside for highlights on the fabric.

5 Remove the stencil and, lastly, paint the stamen with yellow paint.

PAINT
Grass green
Brown
Maroon
Yellow
Opaque white
Purple

SILKSCREEN PRINTING

Silkscreen printing developed from the Japanese technique in which silk is stretched very tightly over a wooden frame, the negative of a pattern is applied to the fabric and the pattern is then transferred to an article by forcing the paint through the holes in the fabric. Today we do not use silk any more, but prefer stronger and cheaper materials such as nylon and polyester *inter alia*. Silkscreen printing can be an expensive and highly technical process if you are planning to do intricate printing, but in this chapter we are going to concentrate on only a few inexpensive and simple techniques.

Nowadays, silkscreen printing is often used commercially for printing curtaining and dress fabrics. Many small businesses also use the process to print T-shirts, table mats and tablecloths *inter alia*. In this case, silkscreen printing is an expensive and highly technical process. There are, however, cheaper and simpler techniques that you can use at home. With these techniques you can repeat the same pattern perfectly, and you can use a fairly intricate pattern. There is also no need for bridges in the design as is necessary for stencilling.

DESIGNS FOR SILKSCREEN PRINTING

You always set out the design for silkscreening on paper first. You can also easily make any changes on the paper until you are completely satisfied. The designs can be very simple or highly intricate, especially if you are using more than one colour and more than one silkscreen per design. In this book, however, we are only going to use simple designs.

MAKING THE SILKSCREEN

REQUIREMENTS
- 40 x 40 mm strong, straight wood
- medium-gauge mesh

1 The measurements of the silkscreen frame will differ according to the size of the design. Keep in mind, however, that the frame must be 10 cm larger on all four sides than the planned design. For our purposes, we need a rectangular frame and the lengths of the sides should be 78 cm and 45 cm respectively.

2 Apply glue to the edges of the individual sides, stick them together and then attach the wood securely with nails or screws. Take care that the frame is firm and unable to bend, and that it lies flat.

3 You can purchase fabric for the frame at most hobby shops that stock textile paint. It is very important that the fabric allows the paint to flow through evenly and smoothly. Carefully cut the fabric 10 cm larger than the frame all round.

4 Wet the fabric thoroughly. Carefully place it over the frame and use a heavy-duty staple gun to staple the fabric to the frame. You can put strips of cardboard on the frame and staple them with the fabric to prevent the fabric at the corners of the frame from tearing. It is much easier if two people work together to attach the fabric to the frame – one person pulls the fabric until it is taut and the other uses the staple gun to fasten it to the frame. The success of the frame depends on how tightly and evenly the fabric is stretched over the frame. Start in the middle of one long side and apply the staples 5 mm apart, at an angle of 45°, onto the wood. Then attach the fabric to the two short sides and to the first long side. Lastly, attach the second long side. There are also other ways of doing this, but this method is the simplest and works very well.

5 Use a squeegee to spread the paint over the fabric and to force it through the fabric. You can also buy this at hobby shops. Make sure, however, that it is narrower than the inner edge of the frame, but bigger than the design. It is best to compare the measurements of the design with those of the ready-made squeegees before you start, as it is much easier to buy one than to have to make one yourself.

METHODS OF TRANSFERRING DESIGNS TO THE SILKSCREEN

There are many methods of transferring the design to the silkscreen. We will discuss only three.

The painting-out method

I prefer to use this particular method because it is easy and cheap. The only things you need to transfer the design to the screen are a small tin of sanding sealer and a smallish brush.

1 Draw a design on paper that is at least 10 cm smaller all round than the inside of the frame.

2 Place the pattern on a flat work surface and place the silkscreen with the fabric onto the pattern.

Silkscreen printing in black on a plain, white background.

3 Using a pencil, trace the pattern onto the fabric.

4 Then lift the screen and hold it at an angle so that the fabric does not touch the work surface. Use a little brush to paint sanding sealer on the parts of the pattern that are not going to be printed. The painted areas will therefore not let any paint through.

5 Hold the screen against the light and make sure that all areas that should be closed, are indeed closed. If this is not the case, you should carefully paint out the open areas.

6 Immediately wash the brush well with turpentine to remove all the sanding sealer. If you do not do this before the brush dries, the bristles will become hard and the brush will not be able to be used again.

7 Allow the sanding sealer to dry thoroughly.

8 If there is more than one colour in the design, make more than one silkscreen and apply it after the first one on the desired surface. However, plan the register, namely where and how the colours are to be applied, very carefully.

Photographic method

When you use a photographic process, you can transfer more intricate patterns, which can even include lettering, to the silkscreen. There are many specialized studios and workshops that do this. It is an expensive process, however, but if there are not too many colours involved, it is still affordable. Remember, the more colours there are in the design, the more expensive it's going to be, because each new colour needs a new silkscreen. To save costs, it might be better to have a detailed design printed in one colour and paint in all the other colours later on.

1 Using a black pen, draw the design on tracing paper. Remember, the design must be about 10 cm smaller than the inside edge of the frame.

2 Make the frame in the desired size and take it with the design to the studio. The silkscreen is then prepared further by them.

After making the design for this calendar, it was transferred to the silkscreen by a reproduction house. The calendar part was done on a computer and printed and enlarged to suit the rest of the design, which was drawn in ink on paper and coloured in with black ink. The calendars can be printed in one colour, just like this example, and you can paint in colours later on.

Designs with paper

This is the simplest and cheapest way to print designs. You make the designs on blank newsprint and then suction the design to the silkscreen with the paint. The disadvantage of this method, however, is that you can only use the design a couple of times. When you have made the planned number of prints, remove the paper design from the frame and wash the frame thoroughly.

1 Use a screen without any pattern for this method.

2 Cut out a rectangular piece of paper, which fits the silkscreen exactly.

3 Tear or cut the design of your choice from the paper and then place the paper on a fabric remnant.

4 Place the screen with its stretched fabric face-down on the paper pattern. The screen now looks like a rectangular container lying on the paper.

5 Pour the paint into the silkscreen at the side farthest from you and take the squeegee and place it behind the paint.

6 Bend forward and pull the paint towards you while holding the screen firmly. If the screen moves, the paint will smudge.

7 The paper pattern is suctioned onto the silkscreen and, when the frame is lifted, the pattern will cling to the bottom of the frame so that it can be used over and over again only for prints in the original colour.

PREPARATION OF THE WORK SURFACE

For silkscreen printing, you need a firm, flat surface that is not too high. Cover the surface with sponge or even an old blanket and attach it firmly to the underside with thumb tacks, so that it cannot move. You can stretch a strong piece of plastic or PVC over the sponge or blanket. If you use plastic, you can treat the area with adhesive spray before the fabric is placed over it. Use very little glue, however, so that the fabric does not become wet. Clean the work surface thoroughly after every job.

CARING FOR YOUR SILKSCREEN

1 Wash the screen very well with water after use.

2 Make sure that all paint is removed and does not remain between the holes of the fabric on the frame. Any paint that dries there will never come out and can change and even ruin the pattern.

3 Pack your frames away from any sharp objects. Even a small slit or hole will spoil your silkscreen, as paint will get through and so weaken the tension of the fabric.

THE PRINTING PROCESS

1 Remember first to wash and shrink the fabric before fabric painting is applied to it.

2 Use black or navy blue for the design. The navy blue is not as hard as the black.

3 Paste a piece of cellophane on one side of the table and place the frame on top of the cellophane. Mark the corners of the frame on the cellophane and make the first print on the cellophane. In this way, the register (or the layout of the design on the fabric) can be planned very carefully.

4 Then place the silkscreen in the desired position on top of the fabric.

5 Pour the paint into the frame at the point farthest away from you.

6 Dip the squeegee in the paint, bend forward and pull the paint over the screen towards you. Make sure that the paint goes everywhere on the pattern.

7 Carefully lift the screen and repeat the process on another part of the fabric. The paint stays wet for a long time, so be careful not to touch the printed parts.

8 It also looks wonderful when more than one colour is used in the printing process. If you decide to use different colours, you must always make sure that the previous layer of paint is completely dry before printing a second colour.

All the equipment you need for silkscreen printing: a silkscreen, a squeegee and a range of paints.

DIFFERENT
types of fabric

Since we usually paint on ordinary cotton, in this chapter we are going to look at examples of fabrics that are used less often. One example is organza, which cannot be fixed by heat, but which looks stunning. Another fabric that is not usually washed is silk. Silk is wonderful to work on because it is a natural material. Then we'll look at thinly woven canvas, which is strong but quite

difficult to paint on; seedcloth, which is available in a few different widths; versatile denim and mattress ticking, on which colours dry brightly, and linen, on which large, earthy designs look fantastic.

ORGANZA

In this example, we did stencilling on a curtain, which is used just as a decoration. Since organza burns very easily, the paint cannot be fixed by heat and so the curtain cannot be washed. It is also very difficult to work with because it is so smooth and slippery. But the end result is marvellous.

If your curtain definitely has to be washable, you could use cotton organza. The effect will not be as ethereal, but the paint can be fixed by heat.

1 Spray the cleaned, firm work surface with a little adhesive spray and press the fabric over it firmly and smoothly, making sure there are no folds or wrinkles.

2 Cut out a rectangular stencil of 10 cm x 25 cm from a piece of plastic (see pages 44–46). We are going to use this rectangular stencil using opaque white paint to make random right angles on the fabric, which in their turn will serve as background for the leaves that will be stencilled on later. The opaque paint also takes better on the organza than the transparent paint, and since the fabric itself has a light beige colour, it will allow the leaves to show up well.

3 Lightly spray the back of the stencil with adhesive spray and place it in the desired position on the fabric. Using a roller, first roll the opaque white paint on a remnant until it has a fine texture before rolling it onto the fabric. Carefully lift the stencil, wash it very well and place it in the next chosen position. Stencil the following block with the roller and opaque white paint.

4 The fabric will have to be moved as you progress. Remember, the paint seeps right through the organza onto the work surface, so make sure that the work surface is clean and dry before putting the fabric on it again.

5 Allow all the white blocks to dry thoroughly before you start stencilling the leaves. However, remember to lift the fabric every so often before the blocks are quite dry, or it may stick to the work surface and tear when you want to remove it.

6 In the example alongside, I turned the fabric over and stencilled the leaves on the back of the white blocks.

The feathers were first stencilled onto the organza, which was then placed over synthetic silk to make up the cushion.

7 Spray the stencils of the leaves lightly with adhesive spray again so that they do not move around, and use flat brushes with different shades of brown to stencil the leaves on the white blocks. It looks most interesting when you stencil the leaves at random without a specific pattern. You can also use a little turquoise paint here and there on the leaves to make the curtain more interesting.

8 Since the fabric is transparent, the edges must be finished very meticulously. Make a neat hem by pulling the threads and then folding, or leave them raw if the fabric is not inclined to unravel. You could also finish the edges with satin ribbon.

SILK

Natural silk fabrics have a wonderful gloss and it is glorious painting on them. Unfortunately, the gloss disappears on those parts of the fabric that have been painted, as well as when it is wet. So paint only on part of the fabric so that the lovely gloss is still visible on the end product.

Silk is very sensitive to heat so the fabric paint cannot be fixed using heat treatments. For this reason, use silk only for those articles that do not need to be washed, such as scatter cushions, which are placed in a room that is not used by children.

1 Using a pencil, trace the design of a rosebud onto the fabric.

2 Begin painting on the silk with a little bit of magenta to which a lot of transparent base has been added. Since the material is very smooth, at the beginning it may possibly feel that the brush is slipping. You will soon get used to it, however, and quite possibly discover that it is magical to paint on silk.

3 For the shadows and the undersides of the petals, use colours to which more magenta and also a little bit of yellow have been added.

4 Paint the stem and calyx with varying shades of olive green and paint the shadows with dark grass green. Use a touch of the light magenta here and there on the sepals.

This rose has been painted on silk, which is always a pleasure to work on. Remember, however, that the glossy finish of the fabric will disappear in those areas that are painted.

THINLY WOVEN CANVAS

Canvas is a strongly woven fabric with a cotton base. It has a fine herringbone appearance and a slight gloss on one side and looks like ordinary cotton on the other. It is thus very suitable for cushions and paintings. It is usually also very wide, but it is not recommended for tablecloths because it is too thick and too stiff. It is also very difficult to care for. Canvas also has to be shrunk before any fabric painting can be done on it, because even a drop of wet paint can make the fabric pucker.

As a result of the ribbed surface, some people find it difficult to paint on canvas, because it sometimes feels as though the fabric is trying to force your brush in a certain direction. So always do a test on a little remnant to see if you get the desired effect.

1 Wash, iron and cut the fabric. For the example on the right you need a 60 cm x 60 cm square. Lightly mark the border, which is 7 cm wide, with a pencil. Using a pencil, trace the design onto the fabric.

2 First paint the fruits. Decide where the highlights will fall on each fruit and leave the natural colour of the fabric to show through there.

3 Use the lightest colours first, namely yellow for the apple and the lightest ochre for the peaches, orange for the cherries and a very light purple for the plums. Always paint the light colours over a larger area than will be visible on the finished product.

4 Then use the darker colours. Paint the apple in streaks with round brushstrokes to accentuate its shape. Paint red shades from the bottom into the yellow. Use magenta for the darker parts and a mixture of magenta and navy blue for the very darkest parts to accentuate the roundness of the apple and to show that it is stationary and not floating.

5 Paint the peaches with different shades of ochre, orange and orange mixed with a little red.

6 Paint the cherries with the same ochre and a little red and orange, with a touch of magenta here and there.

7 Use different shades of purple to paint the plums.

8 Paint the leaves with shades of green, adding a little yellow to the green and then changing the intensity with transparent base and navy blue. Leaves that are all the same colour look very monotonous and lifeless.

The texture of thinly woven canvas is particularly suited to creating a rich appearance when gold paint is applied to it.

9 Draw and paint the stems and pips in different shades of brown.

10 Stick a strip of masking tape on the inside of the pencil line indicating the border and scrape the border with black paint. Then remove the masking tape and let everything dry completely.

11 Stick a strip of masking tape on the outside of the pencil line indicating the border and paint the background with gold paint. Remember, unlike the other colours, gold cannot be smoothed out with a sponge as it loses its gloss. The brushstrokes will therefore be visible when the end product is dry.

SEEDCLOTH

Seedcloth is a cream-coloured fabric with little brown specks and it looks a lot like linen. It is a mixture of cotton and polyester and must first be washed before you can paint on it. It is delightful painting on this fabric and it is particularly suitable for curtains and tablecloths seeing that it is available in different widths up to 2.3 metres.

The colours will obviously look different compared with those painted on white fabric, but the cream-coloured fabric gives the end product a rich, antique effect.

1 To begin, follow steps 1 to 9 of the example on thinly woven canvas (see page 69).

2 Paint the pears with shades of ochre, a little orange, and ochre mixed with a little green for the outer edges.

3 Stick down a strip of masking tape on the inside of the pencil line, indicating the border, and scrape the border with a rich orange-ochre colour. Remove the masking tape and leave everything to dry completely.

4 Scrape the whole piece of fabric, including the design and border, with light cream paint and leave it to dry completely. This scraped layer of cream finishes the painting beautifully and gives the whole design a very rich appearance.

Seedcloth is especially suitable for an antique look – especially if gold paint is used as a finish.

5 Stick a strip of masking tape on the inside of the ochre border, then stick a second strip of tape 2.5 cm from the first strip, on the outside, to form a band that will be painted in gold.

6 Use a plastic squeeze bottle (outliner) with which you can draw, and outline the fruit in gold.

7 Lastly, paint the gold band with a wide brush.

BLUE DENIM

Denim is being increasingly used in interior decoration and today people are making curtains, upholstery, cushions and many other household articles from it.

Denim is a very strong fabric and doesn't get dirty easily so it is particularly suitable for making aprons, pot holders and tablecloths for use outside. Designs primarily made up of shades of blue look the best on this fabric.

1 Remember to shrink the fabric before use. It will then also be softer and so much easier to work on. After washing, the denim will crease badly, so iron it while it is still damp.

2 You work in a completely different way with dark denim than on the ordinary light fabric that we have used up to now. You must trace the design with white carbon paper onto the denim, or draw it directly on the fabric with a white pencil.

3 Transparent paint will also not show up on the dark denim, so you first need to apply a layer of opaque white paint to the whole design. In the design on the right, the other colours were painted directly onto the wet opaque paint to make lovely shades. You can also wait for the opaque white paint to dry completely before painting other colours onto it, but it is then sometimes quite difficult to get bright colours.

This denim apron, with its designs of fruit in shades of blue and green, is ideal for use outside around the barbecue.

WHITE DENIM

You can use the smooth back side of white denim, which has been previously washed, very successfully for any painting technique. We used a combination of techniques for these curtains: we stencilled the zebra stripes and the feathers; used the same silkscreen that was used for the calendar as the main motif; used the scraping technique for the stripes and the painting technique to colour in the feathers.

1 Plan and measure the curtains carefully before you try to start painting. Clearly mark where the hems are going to be so that the silkscreen motifs will be visible on the front of the curtain and not folded in halfway when the hems have to be sewn.

2 Using a marking pen, draw a line 22 cm from where the hem must be folded in and stick a strip of masking tape to the top of this line. Use black paint and a roller to stencil zebra stripes and leave the paint to dry completely.

3 Draw a second line 10 cm above the border of zebra stripes and stick two strips of masking tape at the outsides of this new 10-cm-wide band. Use a scraper and scrape this band with dark ochre paint. When the paint is dry, use a black pen to draw the porcupine quills on the ochre strip and paint them with black and opaque white paint.

4 Divide the width of the curtain evenly and measure precisely where the silkscreen prints should be before starting with the printing.

5 Print the silkscreen prints with black paint and leave them to dry completely before proceeding.

White denim curtains with a combination of silkscreen printing, stencilling and painting techniques.

6 Plan precisely where the feathers should be stencilled and stencil them with a brush and black paint. The colours get painted in later on.

7 Colour in the silkscreen and feathers with different colours paint. To make the curtain even more interesting, you can sew on real feathers.

MATTRESS TICKING

In the past, this fabric was only used to cover mattresses, hence the name. Fortunately, someone discovered that you can do much more with it and today it is used to make curtains, cushions and covers. It is 100 per cent cotton, strong and particularly suited to painting because the colours dry very brightly on it. Because there are dark blue stripes in the fabric, not all patterns will be suitable for painting on this fabric.

1 Remember always to shrink the fabric before you use it and before you begin painting on it. It will then also be a little softer and so much easier to work on. After it has been washed, the ticking will crease badly, so iron it while it is still damp.

2 For the examples below, the fruits were traced in blue and painted in shades of navy blue and green. We obtained the cheerful blue colours by adding transparent base to navy blue and the fresh greens by adding emerald green and navy blue to the grass green.

This breakfast set made of mattress ticking looks very appealing, with its fruit designs in shades of blue and green.

LINEN

Linen is a natural fibre, which is usually very coarsely woven. Because the fabric is so coarse, large, simple, earthy designs without a background look the best, and small, delicate designs should preferably be avoided.

Linen is usually a light brown, cream or ecru colour and, compared with white fabrics, will have an affect on the way colours show up in the design.

1 Always remember to shrink the fabric before any fabric painting is done. It will then also be softer and so much easier to work with. After it has been washed, the linen will crease badly, so iron it while it is still damp.

2 Trace the outlines of the design onto the linen in black.

3 Mix yellow and magenta and lots of transparent base to paint the shadows on the flowers.

4 Use opaque white to finish off the flowers.

5 Paint the stigmas of the flowers with yellow.

6 Paint the stems with different shades of olive green.

7 Cover the linen with organza when the cushions are completed for a lovely, ethereal effect.

Linen cushions covered with organza bound in silk. The arum lilies have been finished with opaque white, which contrasts beautifully with the ecru background.

DECORATING
around the home

In this chapter, we concentrate on creative ideas for brightening up your home, or even your office.

The projects in this section are fairly advanced. It is assumed that you have already mastered the different techniques in the previous chapters, so they

are not explained in great detail again and the method is also only given in broad terms. If you are in doubt, you should refer to the first couple of chapters that deal with the specific technique.

TABLECLOTH
with indigenous flowers

A design of indigenous flowers looks beautiful on fabric.

For this tablecloth, I used large white daisies together with

smaller blue daisies *(Felicias)* and blue plumbago florets.

PAINT
Magenta
Navy blue
Yellow
Opaque white
Transparent base
Orange
Olive green

1 Using a dark blue pen, trace the outlines of the design onto the fabric. The lines do not have to be the same thickness everywhere, but you get a lovely effect when the lines are fairly thick at the hearts of the flowers.

2 The petals have little folds over the length, so paint the daisies in streaks. Alternate light and dark shades of the colours over the length of the petals for depth.

3 Use magenta, light and dark variations of navy blue and light and dark variations of yellow mixed with magenta to get the pale apricot colour for the large white daisy in the centre. Start painting at the middle of the flower and gradually work outwards so that the shadows in the middle and also where the petals overlap are dark and the rest of the petals are very pale. Then paint with opaque white from the tips and outsides of the leaves towards the inside. Mix the opaque white with some transparent base when you get near to the inside of the leaves so that all the shadowed parts and the white parts flow more gently into each other.

4 Mix navy blue with transparent base for the heavenly blue colour of the border, the plumbago florets and the blue daisies. Use navy blue with less transparent base for the shadows on these flowers, and here and there you can mix a little magenta with the blue to get a blue-purple shade. Remember to leave the highlighted areas open, so that the white of the fabric shows through.

5 The petals of the plumbago florets are smooth and silky and must be painted as such. The paint should therefore be very light and skilfully blended together. Also make sure that there are white highlights on the petals. The hearts of these flowers are not painted at all to let the white of the fabric show through.

A tablecloth with indigenous flowers in white and different shades of blue. The blue in the border accentuates the blue in the flowers.

6 The small white daisies are painted here and there with a little opaque white paint. Paint the hearts of the daisies with dark yellow and orange.

7 Use four shades of olive green for the leaves. Paint the leaves that are at the back darker than those that are in the front and leave white bits of the fabric open so that it looks as though the leaves are shining where the light reflects on them.

8 Scrape a 17-cm-wide border all round in light blue, as discussed on page 33.

MAGNOLIA

This design looks equally good as a tablecloth or as a painting.

PAINT
Transparent base
Yellow
Magenta
Brown
Shades of grass green
Shades of emerald green
Navy blue
Opaque white

1 Use a black pen to trace the outlines of the magnolia onto the fabric. Position the design in the centre of the tablecloth. The tablecloth in this example measures 120 cm x 120 cm.

2 Mix a couple of very light ochre shades using yellow and magenta and lots of transparent base. You can get the different shades by varying the proportions of the yellow and magenta. To paint in shadows on the flower, use the darkest shades where the petals meet in the middle and also where their leaves fold. Also use a little brown here and there on the edges of the petals. Vary the shades to give the flower depth and life and use a little green in the central part of the flower.

3 Paint the stamens with the darker and orange-ochre colours.

4 Use shades of grass green and emerald green and a little ochre here and there to paint the leaves in front. Mix emerald green with navy blue for the leaves at the back and for the darkest parts of the leaves near to the veins and against the petals.

5 Use shades of brown and a touch of green to paint the stem. Allow the paint to dry completely.

6 Mark the outer edge of the central block 19 cm from the side of the tablecloth and stick a strip of 2-cm-wide masking tape at the outside of the line. The strip of masking tape serves as a boundary on the inside for the central cream-coloured block and on the outside as a boundary for the outermost green border.

A tablecloth with a single magnolia. The yellowish-cream colour
that is scraped over the centre block creates a soft, antique look.

7 Mix a very pale yellowish-cream colour and scrape from the middle of the strip of masking tape to the middle of the centre block. Scrape this paint over the whole block, including the flower.

8 Now use the opaque white paint while the cream paint is still wet and paint the edges and lightest parts of the petals again. Also mix transparent base with the opaque white for the softer, shadowed parts.

9 Scrape the outside border of the design with a light yellow-green shade.

TABLECLOTH with white poinsettias

This spectacular tablecloth with its white poinsettia design is ideal for Christmas.

PAINT
Dark green
Yellow
Ochre
Reddish-brown
Opaque white
Transparent base
Gold
Navy blue

1 Using dark green, neatly trace the outlines of the poinsettias onto the fabric at the four corners of the tablecloth. Use a plastic squeeze bottle, the kind used for drawing, for tracing the design.

2 Paint the petals at the top with light olive green, a little light yellow-green and a little bit of ochre. Use less light green and more and more ochre and reddish-brown the further the leaves are to the back.

3 Use opaque white to paint over the parts of the large petals that are already painted. Paint from the outside to the inside. The nearer to the veins, the more opaque white should be mixed with transparent base, and blended into the other shadow colours.

4 Paint the leaves with shades of olive green that have been lightened with some transparent base. Lastly, add a little yellow to the lightest olive green to get a light, bright green.

5 Stick down a 2-cm-wide strip of masking tape to get the white strips of the border between the dark green background and the golden central part of the tablecloth.

6 Mix a little bit of olive green with navy blue to get a nice dark green for the background area between the leaves.

7 Paint the central part of the tablecloth gold, as well as the bits between the flowers on the long sides of the outer edge. Use a scraper for this and a brush where the scraper cannot reach. Do not try to smooth the gold paint with a sponge, since the gloss will disappear.

A tablecloth with white poinsettias for a merry Christmas dinner. If you want red flowers, use shades of a very bright orange-red colour. Magenta can be added for very dark flowers.

PAINTINGS with tulips

This is an example of a simple pattern that is divided into three and from which three paintings are made. The paintings are framed without mounting in thin gold frames. The paint is largely applied using the scraping method and the flowers are highlighted with opaque white paint. Remember, the feeling and atmosphere of a painting depends a lot on the amount of detail. The more detail, the more realistic the painting. You decide how realistic or abstract you want it to be.

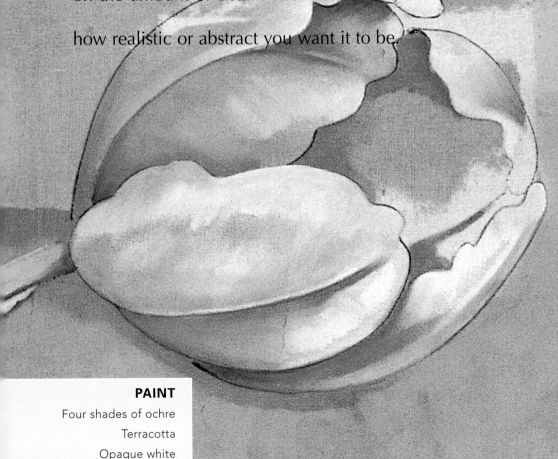

PAINT
Four shades of ochre
Terracotta
Opaque white

1 The visible part of each of the frames in this example measures 47 cm x 76 cm. The pattern must therefore be at least 149 cm x 84 cm [(47 x 3) + 8 cm] x [(76 + 8) cm]. Divide the pattern into three equal parts, marking these divisions with a pencil line. Draw another two lines 4 cm on both sides of the dividing line. These lines determine up to where the pattern will be traced, since

A painting that extends over three pictures: the design is interrupted, but no part of it is omitted.

each painting is at least 4 cm larger all round than what is visible after it is framed. If this is not done, it will look as though there is a hole in the pattern. Therefore, the pattern will cross at the parts where it is divided.

2 Trace the design in black onto the fabric. Remember that the painting on the left-hand side is going to have 4 cm on the right-hand side that is the same as the first 4 cm visible on the left-hand side of the middle painting, so that it is visible right up to the dividing line when it is framed. In the same way, the middle painting will have the last 4 cm on the right-hand side that is the same as the first 4 cm visible on the left-hand side of the right-hand painting.

3 Paint the background using the scraping technique and five different colours paint. Use a scraper about 18 cm wide. Plan approximately where and how the colours are going to be applied. Usually, the lightest

colours are applied to the outsides, at the top and on the flowers, with darker colours being applied where depth is required. The white fabric, too, is clearly visible in certain places. This gives added texture and depth to the painting. Use the outlines of the design as a guide to decide where a certain colour will end. Always start scraping with the lightest colour and then work from light to dark. You can get interesting effects by scraping the colours over each other in places.

4 Although these paintings are not realistic, it looks splendid when the flowers and leaves in the front of the paintings are spotlighted. While the scraped paint is still wet, you can immediately start to create accents in some places by applying opaque white paint, particularly on the tips of the leaves. Also mix the opaque white with a little ochre paint to lift out certain light parts of the flowers. Paint the parts between the leaves darker to get even more depth.

PAINTINGS for the kitchen

Make your own wooden frames – it's an inexpensive

and easy way to frame your painted fabrics.

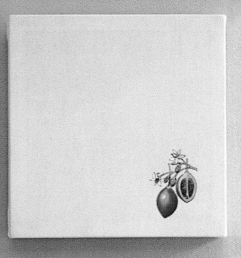

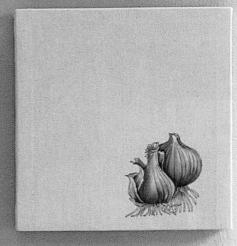

WOODEN BOX FRAMES

REQUIREMENTS

- Fabric with the design already painted true on it. Remember, use a strong fabric, which is preferably woven true, and ensure that the fabric measures at least 5 cm larger all round than the completed frame. The measurements of these examples are 60 cm x 60 cm. The size of the fabric will, therefore, be 70 cm x 70 cm to make provision for the fabric being pulled over the edges and stapled to the back.
- Square-cut wood 2.5 cm x 2.5 cm x the respective length of the sides, or strong skirting boards. You can use any type of wood that does not warp and is without cracks, such as good-quality pine or meranti. The measurements will also depend on the eventual size of the frame. You will need thicker wood for a very large artwork.
- Staple gun and staples
- Joiner's glue
- Nails

1 Decide how big the framed article is going to be and then add twice the thickness of the frame all round. Therefore, if the frame is 2.5 cm wide, 5 cm is added all round. Make sure that the corners are square – remember, a skew piece of fabric cannot be pulled straight later on. If you work correctly from the start, you will save yourself a lot of bother.

2 Using a pencil, draw a guideline on the reverse side of the fabric. This line is drawn at a distance that is twice the width of the frame, from the outer edge of the fabric. Carefully iron folds into the fabric along these lines. These folds will then serve as a guide for the outlines of the finished article. Trace the design onto the fabric and then paint it. Leave the paint to dry completely.

3 Iron the fabric on the wrong side to fix the paint. Each side of the frame is the width of the wood shorter than the finished length of the side. In the case of the examples, where the sides are 60 cm long and the wood is 2.5 cm wide, each piece of wood is therefore 57.5 cm long. Stick the wood together with joiner's glue and then attach the two pieces of wood on each corner with two nails as well. Allow the glue to dry completely.

4 Take care that the ironed folds, which should still be slightly visible, lie on the outer edge of the frame. Firmly staple the first side of the fabric to the back – but leave the last 5 cm of the sides loose so that you can make neat folds at each corner.

5 Staple the next side and keep on until all four sides are stapled.

6 Fold the corners flat and staple down.

BOX FRAME WITH FIGS

1 Trace the outlines of the figs onto the fabric in black, and then trace the leaves in the background with a pencil.

2 For the whole fig, we spotlight the shape by painting the top of the fig and the curves lighter than the bottom and the grooves. The colours are applied on top of each other, so do not be scared to paint whole areas light blue and then paint over them with the darker bluish-purple shades, working from the bottom. Even the green and light ochre are painted over the light blue.

3 The little seeds visible in the cut fig are painted in variations of magenta. Leave highlights open on the seeds so that the white of the fabric shows through.

PAINT
Transparent base
Navy blue
Purple
Grass green
Ochre
Magenta
Opaque white

A painting of figs stretched over a wooden box frame. The outlines of the figs are traced in black ink and the leaves in the background are traced in pencil.

4 Then paint the sections between the skin and the pips with opaque white.

5 Scrape the background of the painting with a very light shade of green.

6 Paint the leaves and the shadows in the background with different shades of green and ochre.

BOX FRAME WITH POMEGRANATE

1 Neatly trace the outlines of the pomegranates in black pen onto the fabric, and trace the leaves and flowers in the background in pencil.

2 Paint the pips with varying shades of magenta. First use the lighter shades and leave highlights open where the white of the fabric shows through so that the pips look round. Lastly, use the darker shades on the outsides of the pips.

3 Paint the whole pomegranate, using light ochre, especially at the top. Then use shades of red, magenta and lastly green on the shadowed side to build up the colours of the skin. Let the colours overlap so that there are are many interesting variations. In the dark section right at the bottom, for instance, dark magenta and dark green provide a very interesting shadow.

4 Now paint the skin of the cut pomegranate with darker shades of red, magenta and green.

5 Paint the membranes between the pips and outer skin with opaque white.

6 Scrape the background with light terracotta and leave it to dry completely.

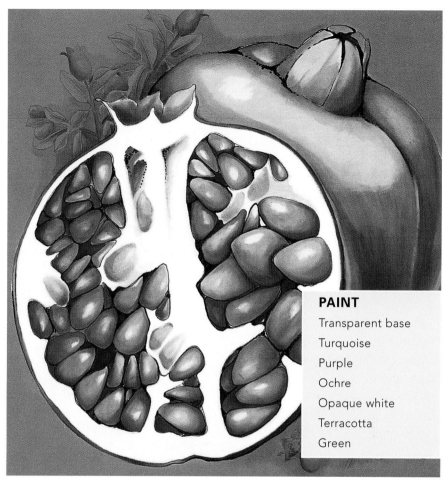

PAINT
Transparent base
Turquoise
Purple
Ochre
Opaque white
Terracotta
Green

A painting of pomegranates stretched over a wooden box frame. The size of the box frame can be adjusted to fit the area where it will be displayed.

7 Use shades of terracotta and green to paint in the little twigs and leaves and pomegranate flowers in the background.

BOX FRAME WITH GARLIC

1 Trace the outlines of the large heads of garlic in black onto the fabric and trace the garlic plants in the background in pencil.

2 Paint the large bulbs of garlic and the clove of garlic with light purple and ochre shades. To emphasize the rough texture and the rounded shape of the garlic, use dark shades for the folds and for the shadows. You can apply the different colours over each other to get some interesting colour variations.

3 Paint opaque white over the wet paint. Place the brush on the light parts first and then paint towards the darker, shadowed areas.

PAINT

Transparent base
Shades of magenta
Shades of ochre
Shades of red
Shades of grass green
Opaque white
Shades of terracotta

A painting of garlic stretched over a wooden box frame. Use dark shades for the folds and shadows to recreate the rough texture of a garlic bulb.

4 Scrape the whole background with a light terracotta and leave it to dry completely.

5 Paint in the garlic plants in the background. Use dark terracotta and green for the bulbs and leaves, and opaque white for the florets and here and there on the leaves.

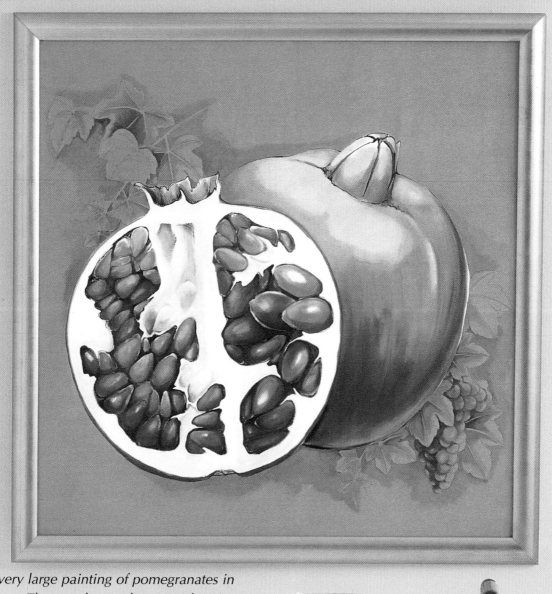

An example of a very large painting of pomegranates in a traditional frame. The membranes between the pips and outer skin are emphasized with opaque white paint.

TABLECLOTH with iceberg roses

Painting and stencilling were used to make this tablecloth.

PAINT
Opaque white
Olive green
Yellow
Transparent base
Navy
Purple
Ochre
Apple green

1 Using a black pen, trace the roses onto the fabric in the centre of the tablecloth.

2 Plan how and where you want to place the stencilled roses around the border. Now stencil the roses with a small roller and opaque white paint right round the border and leave to dry completely.

3 Use olive green paint mixed with a little yellow to scrape a 19-cm border, as described on page 33, over the white stencilled roses. Use a thin brush to paint in the background between the petals and leaves of the large roses in the middle, where it is not possible to use a scraper. Then use a clean sponge to even out and smooth the paint, if you like. Be very careful, however, not to smudge the paint over the middle design.

This tablecloth is a good example of how the painting and stencilling techniques can be successfully combined.

4 Now paint the leaves with a brush in three shades of olive green. Mix the olive green with different amounts of transparent base to get a variety of shades. Start with the lightest shades and then move on to the darker colours. Use the darkest colour for the shadowed sections and remember to leave highlighted areas open, particularly on the edges of these leaves, so that the white material shows through.

5 Paint the shadowed areas of the flowers with light blues, light purples, light ochre and yellow, and add a touch of apple green here and there. Paint the rest of the flowers with the opaque white paint, working from the edges of the petals to the inside shadowed colours. You can use some of the transparent base to blend the white opaque paint with the colours in shadow.

TABLECLOTH
with strawberries and zebra stripes

Strawberries are always a favourite and jolly design for a tablecloth, which when

combined with the zebra stripes has a definite African feel.

PAINT
Black
Primula yellow
Shades of bright red
Magenta
Navy blue
Shades of bright green
Opaque white

1 Cut the fabric of your choice to the desired size and, using a marking pen, mark a 22-cm-wide border right around. Stick a strip of masking tape on the inside of this line so that no black paint reaches the middle block in which the strawberries will be painted.

2 Use a stencil, roller and black paint to stencil the border neatly. First stencil two opposite borders and leave the paint to dry completely. Then stencil the other two sides and leave the paint to dry completely.

3 Stick strips of masking tape to the outside of the lines that were drawn 22 cm from the edge. In other words, the masking tape is stuck over the zebra stripes to prevent you from painting over and between them when you paint the strawberries.

Stencil the border first, then paint the strawberry design in the centre.

4 Using a black pen, trace the strawberries over the whole central block. Start with a strawberry in the middle and then trace the others so that it looks as though they are lying on top of each other from the inside out.

5 First paint the centre strawberry. Use yellow, red and magenta for the strawberries in the middle and a mixture of magenta and navy blue to get a very dark maroon for the darkest strawberries at the back.

6 Paint the stems with light and dark grass green.

7 Lastly, use opaque white to paint the little spots.

8 You can also paint your own crockery to match your tablecloth. To make the tablecloth more interesting, you can paint a variety of fruits among the zebra stripes.

TABLECLOTH with blocks and ethnic border

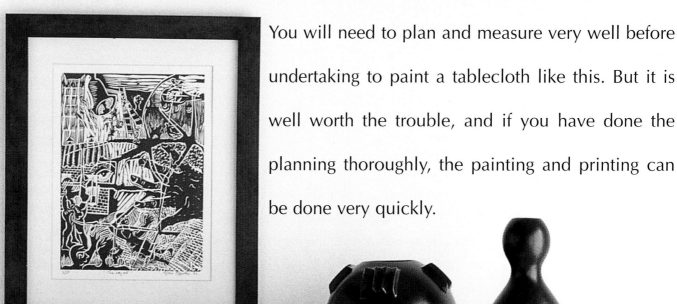

You will need to plan and measure very well before undertaking to paint a tablecloth like this. But it is well worth the trouble, and if you have done the planning thoroughly, the painting and printing can be done very quickly.

PAINT
Gold
Black
Transparent base

1 Decide how big the tablecloth is going to be so that you can work out the size of the blocks and the width of the border relative to those measurements. Try to work with squares with sides between 22 cm and 26 cm and make the white strips about 3 cm wide or as wide as a strip of masking tape. The border is 30 cm wide.

Example:
Tablecloth 180 cm x 180 cm
Border: 30 cm right round
Block in the middle:
120 cm x 120 cm

Mark out four blocks with sides 25 cm each – 20 cm, therefore, remains for white strips. For four blocks, you need five white strips. Make the strips 3 cm each, that is 15 cm. Therefore, add 2.5 cm to each edge and make the width of the border 32. 5 cm.

2 Cut the material to the desired length and mark a border of 32.5 cm right round with a marking pen. Also mark off the blocks and stick down the strips of masking tape.

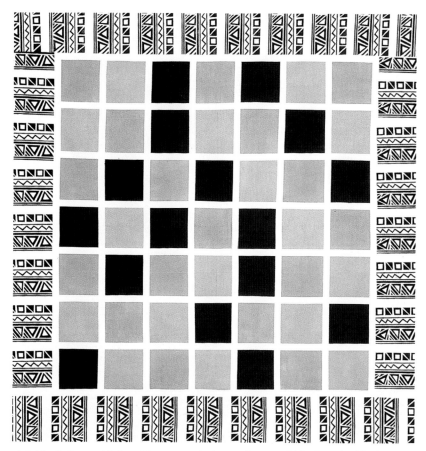

A tablecloth combining silkscreen printing and scraped blocks. The blocks have been coloured randomly to give the tablecloth an informal look.

3 You can now do the silkscreen printing around the border and the scraping of the blocks in the middle. The sequence doesn't matter, but if you are making a very larger tablecloth it is easier to start with the middle blocks. Use a silkscreen and black paint to print the border pattern. First print the two opposite sides. Then print the other two sides – just be careful where the paint is still wet.

4 Now scrape the blocks with gold, black and grey paint. Mix the black paint with lots of transparent base to get grey. You can also use silver instead of grey. The colours don't have to follow a set pattern and can be applied randomly. Sponge the black and grey paint for an even finish, but do not rub the gold or silver paint at all, since they will lose their gloss.

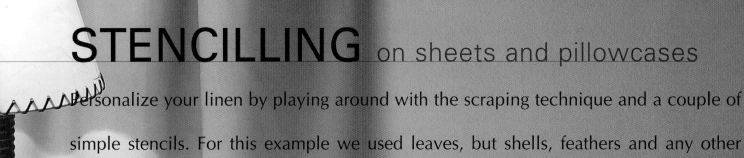

STENCILLING on sheets and pillowcases

Personalize your linen by playing around with the scraping technique and a couple of simple stencils. For this example we used leaves, but shells, feathers and any other stencil designs would look just as good.

PAINT
Shades of ochre
Shades of olive
Brown
Shades of terracotta
Bronze (not transparent)

1 For this project, we used ready-made cotton sheets and pillowcases. You could also use polyester cotton, but since the paint is fixed with heat, they will then not be quite as drip-dry and will have to be ironed. The paint also usually looks brighter on pure cotton.

2 Using a marking pen, carefully measure the strips on the sheet and the blocks on the pillowcases. In the example on the left, the strip on the sheet is 16 cm wide and 7 cm from the side. The block on the pillowcase measures 34.5 cm x 34.5 cm. If you want to decorate quite a few pillowcases, you can use a square piece of cardboard and trace the outlines each time. This will ensure that all the squares are the same size and will save you lots of measuring.

3 Stick masking tape on the lines to the outside of the areas that will be painted.

4 Place a piece of thin wood or glass covered with thin sponge inside the pillowcase so that the paint does not seep through and stain the back of the pillowcase.

5 Paint the area to the inside of the masking tape with a scraper and light ochre paint. Scrape the paint from the masking tape towards the middle. Never move the scraper outwards, since the paint will seep under the masking tape and you will not have clean lines.

6 Leave the background to dry completely before you start stencilling.

7 Follow the general directions for preparing articles for stencilling on page 46.

This tea-cosy and traycloth have been made using stencilled leaves combined with plain scraped panels.

8 Stencil the leaves at random over the painted strip and block as well as on and outside the edges of the block. Use a flat brush to paint the leaves, moving from the stencil to the inside. Use shades of brown, terracotta and ochre to paint approximately half the leaves, and the bronze opaque paint for the rest of the leaves.

9 Other accessories such as tablecloths, tea-cosies and traycloths look very fetching if the middle block is painted grey and a touch of purple is applied here and there to the leaves.

TABLECLOTH with guinea fowl

A combination of techniques is used for this tablecloth.
The guinea fowl are done with silkscreen printing,
the feathers are stencilled and the background
is painted with a sponge roller.

PAINT
Black
Shades of terracotta
Shades of ochre
Olive green
Transparent base

1 Make a silkscreen frame 50 cm x 40 cm and paint the negative of the design on the silkscreen, in other words the part that is not painted, with sanding sealer.

2 Using light pencil marks or a fabric marker, divide the surface of the tablecloth into four blocks of 60 cm x 60 cm. Also draw guidelines 15 cm from the outer edge so that the prints are always this distance from the outer edge of the tablecloth.

3 Print the guinea fowl with black paint on the tablecloth. Be careful when you put two prints next to each other. Place clean paper over the first print so that the wet paint does not smear off onto the frame of the silkscreen and so smudge black paint all over the fabric. Leave the paint to dry well before proceeding. Remember to wash the silkscreen immediately after use.

4 Make a stencil for the feather and paint a few of them at random on the outer edge. Use black paint and a brush, and paint from the edge of the stencil inwards. Leave the innermost parts of the feather open so that the colours of the background can show through there later on.

5 Scrape the border of the tablecloth 12 cm from the edge with terracotta paint.

6 Use the lightest shade of ochre and scrape the whole inside of the tablecloth with it. You also scrape the paint over the silkscreen prints.

7 Use a darker shade of terracotta and a 10-cm-wide roller and roll a border just inside the outer scraped border, with the middle of the roller on the lines that divide the tablecloth into four blocks.

The different shades on the border are created by applying layers of paint using smooth rollers of varying widths.

8 Use a lighter shade of terracotta and roll another border to the inside of the previous strip.

9 Use a 5-cm roller and olive green paint and roll a border inside the outermost border and on top of the first border that was scraped with the wide roller.

10 Paint a narrow green border over the terracotta strips that divide the tablecloth into four blocks to make the blocks stand out more clearly.

IRISES

Decorate a curtain, cushion and painting with these irises as a theme. The painting on page 108 is done using the painting technique. The mounting is also painted in, which not only looks attractive, but also saves costs when the painting is to be framed.

PAINT FOR STRIPES

Olive green
Light purple (mixture of
light blue and purple)
Dark purple (mixture of
magenta and navy blue)

**PAINT FOR IRISES
AND BUTTERFLIES**

Black
Blue
Yellow
Shades of magenta
Shades of olive green
Shades of purple (light and
dark, and with yellow)
Turquoise

CURTAIN AND CUSHION

1 Cut the fabric for the curtain and cushion and plan the position of the silkscreen prints.

2 Scrape a 6-cm-wide border in olive green with a scraper and X-ray film at the bottom of the curtain and right around the front of the cushion.

3 Leave open a strip 30 cm wide at the bottom of the curtain for the printing and scrape the first stripe with an X-ray film above the white strip so that there is a clear division between the white background and the first stripe.

4 Use a long ruler as a guide for the remaining stripes together with scrapers of different widths so that the lines have different widths. Use up all the paint before dipping the scraper into the paint again, so that you get an uneven effect. You also get interesting colours where the lines cross each other.

5 Clean and dry the ruler well each time you lift it up and before using it again. Place it next to the previous stripe and scrape the next line with another scraper of a different width, so that the width of the lines differs. Repeat this process until all the horizontal lines have been painted. Leave the paint to dry completely before you start with the vertical lines.

6 Scrape the vertical lines in the same way. Use a wide scraper for the light purple lines and a narrow scraper for the dark purple lines. If you want to do cushions, the fabric at the back must be scraped in the same way.

7 Now use black paint and a silkscreen to print the irises and butterfly on the fabric. You can also draw the design in black on the fabric – it takes a long time, however, and the outlines will not be very sharp.

8 Use the rest of the paint in the silkscreen to scrape approximately 30 cm extra fabric black to round off the cushion.

9 Leave the paint to dry completely and then paint the irises, leaves and butterfly with a very fine brush. To emphasize the folds and creases in the petals, paint with many contrasting colours and also different shades of the colours directly next to each other. Visible brushstrokes also give more texture to the petals. Just take care that they go in the right direction. Paint the leaves smooth and without brushstrokes. Colour in the butterfly with turquoise paint.

10 Finish the cushion with black binding.

PAINTING

1 Carefully measure and mark the outer edge of the painting using a pencil. Make sure that the corners are all exactly 90° because the sides must be absolutely equal in width to the frame.

2 Fit the design into the 'frame' and trace the outlines of the flowers in front onto the fabric in black. The leaves in the background are painted in later so that they look softer and create an illusion of distance.

3 Stick masking tape all around the outside of the edge, right up to the petals and leaves that overlap the edge, to prevent the paint from getting into the 'mounting' that we are going to paint.

4 In this painting we want to capture the character of a specific flower and its leaves. The petals are delicate and thin, yet a little creased, while the leaves are hard and smooth and slightly streaky. The folds and creases in the petals are indicated by using many contrasting colours and also different shades of the colours directly next to each other. Also leave clear brushstrokes when you paint to give even more texture to the petals. Make sure that they are in the right direction. The leaves in their turn are painted smoothly and without brushstrokes.

5 Remove the masking tape after the flowers and leaves are painted and are completely dry, and now stick it to the inside of the dividing line between the painting and the 'mounting'. Use ochre paint and scrape the border, which is going to look like mounting, from the inside to the outside. Apply the ochre paint with a fine brush to the flowers and leaves in front of the mounting. Again, allow the paint to dry completely.

PAINT

Blue

Yellow

Green

Gold

Magenta

Ochre

This painting's mounting has also been painted in.

6 Stick a second strip of masking tape 1 cm from the first strip of masking tape right around the outside. There is now a 1-cm-wide strip between the two strips of masking tape that is going to be painted gold to create the illusion of a narrow inner frame.

7 Paint the strip between the two tapes gold.

NASTURTIUMS

1 Using a pencil, neatly trace the design onto the material.

2 The petals have lots of folds and creases and, to get this particular effect, you will need to use a combination of light and dark colours together. The white of the fabric is used for those parts that the light falls upon in the flowers at the top, and a very light yellow-orange and some white spots that show through are used for the darker flowers at the bottom. Use the yellow and orange colours for the flower at the top, lots of orange and light red, orange and very red, and lastly orange, red and very dark red for the flower at the bottom. Mix magenta with a little navy blue to get the darkest red.

3 Paint the seeds and stems with shades of light ochre mixed from magenta, yellow and lots of transparent base.

PAINT
Transparent base
Yellow
Orange
Red
Magenta
Navy blue
Ochre
Shades of green

This display of nasturtiums is portrayed in strong, rich and dark colours.

4 Paint the stems and sepals in shades of green that have been lightened with yellow and plenty of transparent base.

5 No background is painted in.

VASES

Here you use the simplest stencil pattern, used in the explanation of the roller technique in stencilling, to make superb decorations for the wall as well as an unusual tablecloth with checks. You can change the colours to suit your own colour scheme, such as variations of green, different shades of yellow and red, and so on. Remember to mix enough paint and to paint all the articles at the same time, assuming you are making more than one article for the same room.

PAINT FOR PAINTINGS
Shades of blue
Silver

PAINT FOR TABLECLOTH
Purple
Shades of blue
Silver

PAINTINGS

1 Cut two pieces of fabric measuring 48 cm x 68 cm. The completed paintings are 36 cm x 56 cm, but 6 cm is allowed all round for folding when framing.

2 Using a pencil, mark the edge to be painted silver 9 cm from the fabric edge. This border will be used instead of mounting and rounds off the painting well. Then scrape the fabric for the area to be painted with very light blue paint.

3 Stencil a vase on each piece of fabric as described on page 49.

4 Stick masking tape at the inside of the line indicating the border and scrape the border with silver.

TABLECLOTH

1 Using a purple marker, mark the edges of the checked border. For a tablecloth 120 cm x 120 cm, the outer border is 7 cm wide, the checked border is 30 cm wide and the middle block is 46 cm x 46 cm.

2 Stick masking tape between the outside border of the tablecloth and the checked border and the central block so that the checks do not encroach on the border or central block. Paint the checks as shown on page 34.

3 The 6-cm-wide purple stripes and the 2.5-cm and 3-cm royal blue stripes, which alternate with 2.4-cm gaps, are made in one direction. The 3-cm-wide cross stripes alternate every 2.3 cm and then 3.3 cm and are the same colour as the vases.

Stencilling and checks are combined on this tablecloth.

4 Let the checks dry. Scrape the whole tablecloth with very light blue paint and leave to dry completely.

5 Stick a strip of masking tape to the inside of the line between the checks and the outermost border of the tablecloth. Scrape the border with royal blue paint.

6 Decide on the position of the vases and stencil them as described on page 49.

7 Stick masking tape between the central block and the checked border. Stick another strip 2 cm to the inside of this block and paint the gap between them with silver.

8 Finish the edge of the tablecloth with an overlocker or sew a neat hem.

PATTERNS

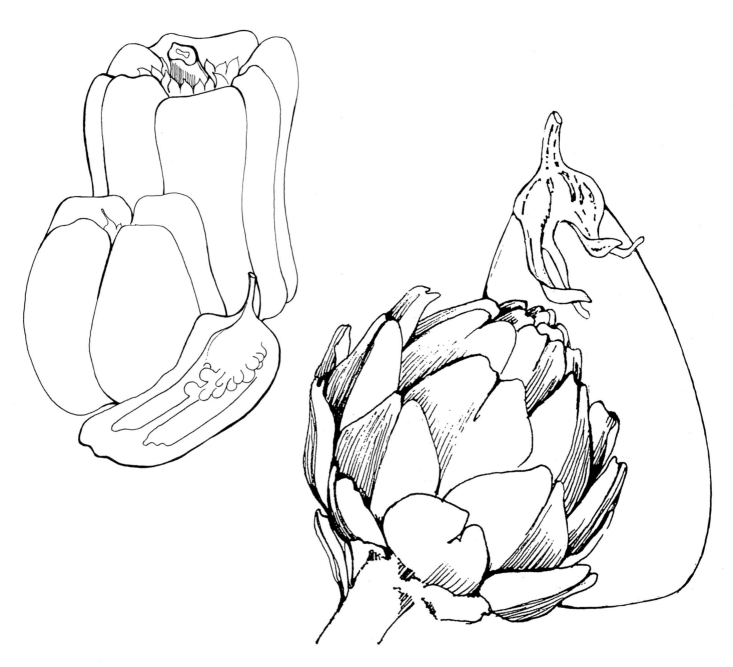

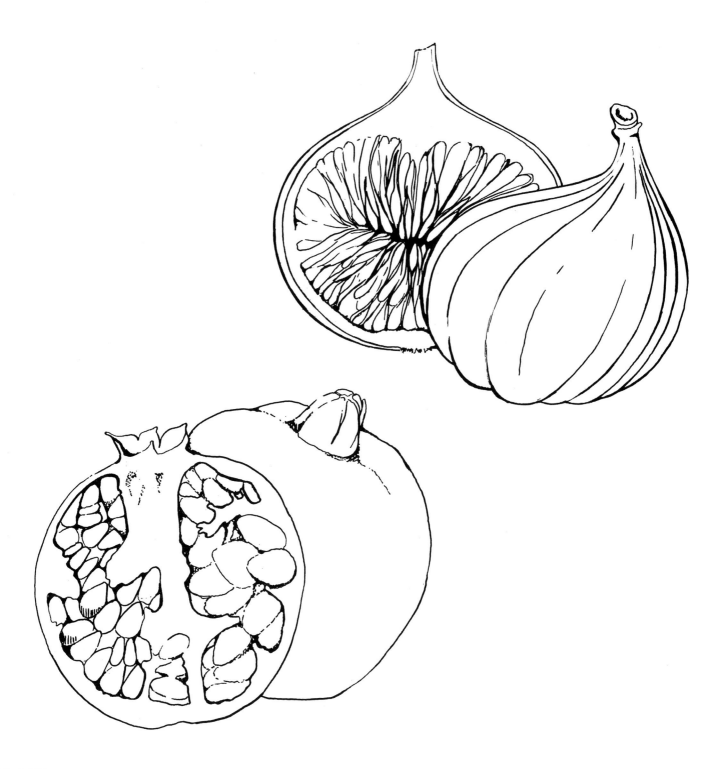

INDEX

(Page numbers in **bold** indicate photographs)

First published in the UK in 2003 by
New Holland Publishers (UK) Ltd
Garfield House
86–88 Edgware Road
London W2 2EA
United Kingdom
www.newhollandpublishers.com
London • Cape Town • Sydney • Auckland

2 3 4 5 6 7 8 9 10

PUBLISHING MANAGER: Linda de Villiers
EDITOR: Manette Lambrechts
DESIGNER: Beverley Dodd
DESIGN ASSISTANT: Sean Robertson
PHOTOGRAPHERS: Warren Heath and Craig Fraser
STYLIST: Sonya Nel

ENGLISH EDITION
EDITOR: Joy Clack
DESIGNER: Beverley Dodd
PROOFREADER: Sean Fraser
Translated into English by Sylvia Grobbelaar from
Stap Vir Stap Lapverfwerk

The authors and publishers wish to thank the following
outlets for their kind assistance and the loan of props for the
photography: House and Interiors, Bright House, City Living,
Deckled Edge and Loft Living.

Reproduction by Hirt & Carter Cape (Pty) Ltd
Printed and bound by Sing Cheong Printing Company Limited

ISBN 1 84330 467 8